More

MAKE IT Fast, COOK IT Slow

Also by

Stephanie O'Dea

. . . .

MAKE IT FAST, COOK IT SLOW:

The Big Book of Everyday Slow Cooking

More

MAKE IT Fast, COOK IT Slow

200 BRAND-NEW, *Budget-Friendly,* SLOW-COOKER Recipes

Stephanie O'Dea

HYPERION

New York

Library of Congress Cataloging-in-Publication Data

O'Dea, Stephanie.
    More make it fast, cook it slow / Stephanie O'Dea.
        p. cm.
    ISBN 978-1-4013-1038-7
1. Electric cookery, Slow. 2. Low budget cookery. I. Title.
    TX827.O36 2010
    641.5'884—dc22
            2010020916

Hyperion books are available for special promotions, premiums, or corporate training. For details contact the HarperCollins Special Markets Department in the New
York office at 212-207-7528, fax 212-207-7222, or email spsales@harpercollins.com.

Book design by Shubhani Sarkar

FIRST EDITION

10   9   8   7   6   5   4   3   2   1

THIS LABEL APPLIES TO TEXT STOCK

We try to produce the most beautiful books possible, and we are also extremely concerned about the impact of our manufacturing process on the forests of the world
and the environment as a whole. Accordingly, we made sure that all of the paper we
used has been certified as coming from forests that are managed to ensure the pro-
tection of the people and wildlife dependent upon them.

To my
**THREE
BEAUTIFUL GIRLS:**
I love you
so very much

CONTENTS

INTRODUCTION *1*

$7 and *Under*

BEVERAGES *15*

BREAKFASTS *19*

APPETIZERS *23*

SOUPS & STEWS *30*

BEANS *41*

SIDE DISHES *54*

VEGETARIAN MAIN COURSES *67*

POULTRY *81*

BEEF & PORK *87*

DESSERTS *94*

$10 and *Under*

BEVERAGES *108*

BREAKFASTS *112*

APPETIZERS *119*

SOUPS & STEWS *125*

BEANS *137*

SIDE DISHES 145

VEGETARIAN MAIN COURSES 152

FISH 156

POULTRY 163

BEEF & PORK 177

DESSERTS 193

$15 and *Under*

BEVERAGES 203

BREAKFASTS 206

APPETIZERS 211

SOUPS & STEWS 216

BEANS 227

SIDE DISHES 232

FISH 239

POULTRY 242

BEEF, PORK, LAMB, & VENISON 253

DESSERTS 280

Staples

Staples 288

ACKNOWLEDGMENTS 303

INDEX 305

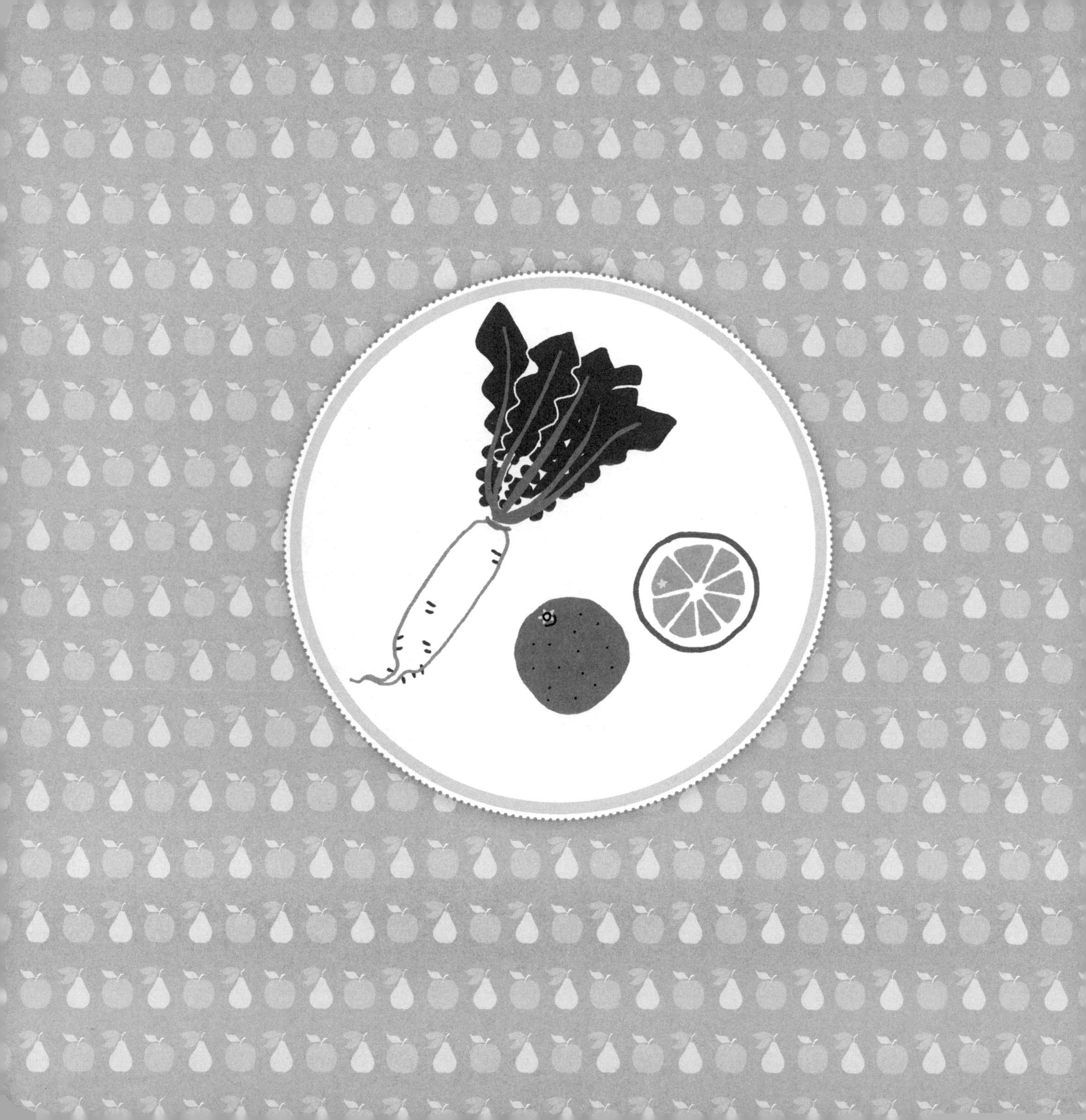

INTRODUCTION

The Back Story

I am not a chef. I have no formal training in anything culinary related, although I have been to quite a few Pampered Chef parties (for the record, the handheld chopper rocks). What I do have is a deep and abiding love for my slow cookers. I got my first slow cooker on my twenty-first birthday, along with a food dehydrator and a pasta machine. I was engaged to be married, and thought I should learn to be a bit more domestic. I had only used the food dehydrator and pasta machine a few times before shoving them into the back of a kitchen cabinet. I found the prep work and ensuing mess daunting, and I wasn't enamored of the shriveled fruit and squishy pasta.

But my slow cooker? My slow cooker gave my domestic side a much-needed boost of esteem. This was a machine I could use. I was fascinated with the way this simple device was able to transform a forgotten and frostbitten roast from the back of the freezer into quite a tasty meal. I was amazed at how effortlessly I could throw together soups and stews, and how tender and moist chicken breasts could become when almost completely ignored.

I continued to use my slow cooker through the early years of my marriage, and fell in love with it all over again when I became a mother. I quickly learned that the only way to ensure a proper family dinner at 6:00 PM was to get the slow cooker loaded up early in the morning while I was still caffeinated and coherent. It just wasn't safe to chop vegetables during the afternoon "witching hours" with cranky kids hanging from my ankles, and once my children hit school age, we spent our afternoons and early evenings at scout meetings or on the sports field. Slow cooking became a way of life.

In January of 2008, I took my love of the slow cooker to the Internet. I began working for BlogHer ads.com, and knew that in order to better understand my job, I should begin a blog. I was hesitant to share too many personal details with the Internet, and liked the idea of a food blog. But I didn't really know how to cook—I just liked to use my slow cookers! When I joked with my husband that I should make a New Year's resolution to use my slow cooker daily and write about it online, Adam told me to "go for it." On January 1, 2008, A Year of Slow Cooking was born.

When I began my yearlong adventure, I didn't think I would come up with new recipes or uses for the slow cooker, and I didn't think anyone reading along at home would attempt to make any of the food I presented. This changed on Valentine's Day, 2008, when I made a perfect crème brûlée at home, in my tiny kitchen, in the slow cooker. I was thrilled that this delicate dessert came out so well, and decided to e-mail the Rachael Ray television show to share my discovery. A producer called a few weeks later, and I flew to New York to appear in person on the show.

After this appearance, my handful of daily readers grew to a few thousand, and I was asked to assemble the recipes from my yearlong adventure into a book. My first cookbook, *Make It Fast, Cook It Slow: The Big Book of Everyday Slow Cooking* is a compilation of 338 of the very best recipes from my year of slow cooking. I am quite proud of that book, and am overjoyed that I had the opportunity to share my slow cooker experiences with so many people.

While the recipes presented in my first book are delicious, fun, and at times revolutionary, they don't reflect another one of my passions: saving money. Although I can make a fantastic lobster bisque in the slow cooker, this isn't really a practical meal for most busy families. This new book has 200 brand-new recipes that will bridge the gap between being innovative and practical. Although all these dishes fit into a specific budget, I am happy to state that the included recipes do not skimp on flavor—I have chosen hearty, delicious selections, covering all meals from breakfast to dessert. I hope you enjoy it.

Are You Cheap? Frugal? Responsible? Does It Really Matter?

I don't like wasting money. I'm a sucker for a bargain, and have a hard time buying anything without first double-checking the price tag. I've been teased in the past and called "cheap"—and while I used to feel embarrassed, this is now a label I wear proudly. When I first joined the workforce, I kept a loaf of bread in my desk drawer and a jar of peanut butter with my name on it in the communal refrigerator. Instead of joining my coworkers for a daily restaurant or deli lunch, I munched on my bread and peanut butter. I'm not sure exactly how much money I saved by doing this, but I'd guess it to be in the neighborhood of a few thousand dollars.

I have a hard time spending top dollar for items when I know that if I just apply myself, I can usually find the same thing (or something quite similar) at a lesser price at a different store or an online retailer. That said, I'm also practical, and know that I can't really spend a lot of my time hopping around grocery stores hunting for the best deal. Instead, I try my hardest to plan my meals around seasonal fruit and vegetables, and to stock up on meat and other high-priced items when they are on sale at my favorite neighborhood grocery store. I've found that by sticking to the same store and keeping to my list, I fare better than driving to a new store to cash in on an advertised price. Unfamiliar stores encourage aisle wandering, and I'm much more prone to impulse shop at a new-to-me store.

Regardless of your financial situation, I'm sure we all know what it's like to worry about bills and expenses, and to lie awake at night concerned about the future. It's no fun.

I've read an awful lot about trimming expenses from the family budget, and it seems the quickest and easiest way to find a bit of extra wiggle room at the end of the month is to pay attention to your purchases at the grocery store.

Using the slow cooker is a fantastic way to trim the fat from your grocery bills. I appreciate that I can use dried beans and inexpensive cuts of meat. I like that, more often than not, a slow cooker dish provides leftovers I can pack for lunch, or stretch into another family meal by serving it over rice or pasta, or using the bits and pieces as a base for soup. With help from the slow cooker, you can stock the freezer with homemade broth, pasta sauce, and slow cooker "TV Dinners" (page 6). You can freeze your own cooked beans to use in your favorite recipes, and make homemade yogurt and baby food. You can cook a whole chicken for its meal, and then use the carcass for broth. Since I began using my slow cookers daily, I've learned that the average amount of energy used for slow cooking is similar to that of a desk lamp: 75 watts on low, and 150 watts on high. This is much less energy use than an oven, stove, or barbecue requires.

About This Book

There are over 200 brand-new recipes in this book that have not been shared in the first *Make It Fast, Cook It Slow* cookbook. The recipes included have been chosen because they are inexpensive to make. I have separated the book into three sections: $7 and under, $10 and under, and $15 and under dishes. Within each section, there are chapters for beverages, appetizers, soups and stews, side dishes, main courses, and desserts. The main-course selections are bountiful, because I believe this is the most beneficial. I have also included a section I've entitled Staples. This section has recipes from my first book that I felt were important to this one, such as making homemade broth, yogurt, and baby food in the slow cooker.

I live in the San Francisco Bay Area, which happens to be a terribly expensive place to live. The prices in this book are from my own hometown, from my own (regional chain) neighborhood grocery store. I did not use coupons to purchase the food, although I did choose to buy items when they were on sale, and chose store brand items if the per-ounce cost was less expensive than that of the name brand. I rounded up instead of down when determining into which section to place a recipe. I also chose to use store-bought broth when determining prices, instead of making my own (recipes included in the Staples chapter), for price continuity.

Because of this, you may find that by shopping with the store circulars in your area, or by using coupons, or by purchasing meat in bulk at a warehouse store, you can find food at a lower price, and that my prices seem inflated. I'm okay with that! I'd much rather err on the side of overestimating the costs.

In the past many slow cooker meals were made cheaply because they revolved around using canned cream-of-something soup. While I do think there is a place in the world for condensed soup, this book does not have a single recipe that calls for this ingredient. My family doesn't use this product due to allergy and health concerns, and since so many recipes already exist with this key ingredient, I wanted to step away and prove to myself (and others!) that inexpensive slow cooker dishes can be made without it. I am such a sucker for a challenge.

This isn't to say that all the recipes included are completely void of processed and convenience food items. Although I happen to live in California and eat a fair amount of tofu and quinoa, I've got a soft spot in my heart for Velveeta®. And bacon.

This book is a group effort. Scores of readers from all over the world sent me their favorite recipes to try in the slow cooker. Some were traditional slow-cooked meals, and some needed to be tweaked to work in the slow cooker. All the recipes have been tested in my own home kitchen, with my own Crock-Pot® slow cookers, and tasted by my (sometimes picky) family: my husband, Adam, and my two big girls, who were five and eight years old at the time. We had a new baby in the home while I was cooking and preparing these recipes, and while she wasn't able to be an official taste tester, many of the dishes were prepared while wearing her in a front pack—I'm definitely a multitasker!

In order to save on publication fees and keep the purchase price of this book down, I've opted not to include photographs. If you would like to see a finished photo as well as preparation photos, please visit the Web site crockpot365.blogspot.com. Every dish has been well documented.

Please note that children under the age of four should not be given hot dogs, nuts, seeds, popcorn, large chunks of meat, whole grapes, carrots, or any other food that may cause choking.

Everything in This Book Is Gluten-Free

The recipes in this book have been prepared completely gluten-free, due to a family intolerance. If you are not gluten-free, feel free to ignore my notes, or file them away in case you ever need to cook for someone with gluten sensitivity. Gluten is found in wheat, barley, and rye. Oats are off-limits, too, unless they come from a specified gluten-free source. Please read all manufacturer labels carefully; ingredients sometimes change with little or no warning. If you would like to learn more about going gluten-free, please visit the celiac.com and celiac.org Web sites.

Because of this need to cook gluten-free, some of the items I have purchased cost more than their traditionally made and manufactured counterparts. Unless otherwise noted, the prices in this book reflect the gluten-free purchase price, proving that you need not break the bank in order to adhere to a gluten-free diet.

I use the following gluten-free foods and condiments in our home kitchen, which are readily found in neighborhood grocery stores, Trader Joe's, Whole Foods, or at Amazon.com:

Aidell's Sausage and Meatballs (read the labels carefully, as not all varieties are gluten-free)

Betty Crocker Gluten-Free cookie and cake mixes

Bob's Red Mill Certified Gluten-Free Whole Grain Rolled and Steel Cut Oats

Coleman Natural Gluten-Free Chicken Meatballs

Food for Life® brown rice bread

General Mills Rice and Corn Chex cereal

Glutino Pretzels

La Choy soy sauce, sweet-and-sour, and teriyaki sauce

Lea & Perrins Worcestershire Sauce, Made in the USA
(only the U.S.-manufactured is gluten-free)

Pamela's Baking and Pancake Mix (I use this as my all-purpose flour)

Pamela's Amazing Wheat-Free Bread Mix

Redbridge beer (Anheuser-Busch)

San-J Tamari, Wheat-Free

Tinkyada Brown Rice pasta (all sizes, including lasagna noodles)

Trader Joe's Brown Rice pasta

Meal Planning and Other Money-Saving Shortcuts

I'm a meal planner. I wish I wasn't sometimes, because having a meal plan attached to the fridge kind of makes me feel like an obsessive control freak. Except. Having this meal plan ensures that I'm not thinking up meal and snack ideas five to six times a day, every day. It also keeps the kids from rummaging through the cupboards multiple times an hour and keeps me from mindlessly snacking my way through a bag of chocolate chips.

The most dreaded question at the end of the day will always be "What's for dinner?" If you've got a slow cooker plugged in on the kitchen countertop, you have already alleviated this problem. Congratulations! Go one step further and write down all your dinner meals for a week, planning a day off once or twice a week to eat leftovers. Once you've got the hang of meal planning for dinner, work with your family to plan out breakfasts, lunches, and snacks. I think you'll be pleasantly surprised at how this simple idea can save an awful lot of time, money, stress, and even calories.

Keeping a well-stocked freezer will also help save your family's valuable time and money. If you make a large batch of food, plan on serving half of it and freezing the leftovers. I found it very comforting to come home from the hospital with my third little one knowing I had about three weeks of meals ready and waiting in the freezer.

Another one of my favorite ways to stock the freezer is by making what I call "slow cooker TV dinners." To do this, pick out a slow cooker recipe, and instead of loading the meat, vegetables, sauces, and spices into your slow cooker, put it all into a zippered freezer bag. Write any extra directions on the outside of the bag with a permanent marker and plop it into the freezer. The night before, take the bag out of the freezer and thaw it overnight in the refrigerator. Slow cook in the morning as directed in the recipe.

Spices enhance the flavor of meals, and in a lot of instances, the little jars of spices purchased at your local grocery store can be the most expensive purchases on your receipt. I've tried to limit the spices in this book to easily found and reasonably priced varieties, but I'd still suggest buying spices in bulk at warehouse stores, or through online and mail-order catalogs for additional savings. Shopping at neighborhood produce stands and ethnic markets will also garner noticeable savings. If you are new to cooking and have very few spices on hand, I suggest purchasing a stocked spice rack from a department store or bed and bath store. These spice racks usually contain twenty to thirty different varieties of spices, and are quite inexpensive (look for heavily discounted prices during the winter holiday season) for such a large quantity. After using this spice rack for a while, you'll get a feel for your favorite cooking spices and can tailor your grocery store purchases accordingly.

Another way to save money in the kitchen is to make your own broth. I've provided recipes for homemade stock and broth in the Staples section of this book, but you can also save an awful lot by forgoing store-bought broth and using bouillon and water. In the past bouillon cubes received a bad reputation for added sodium, preservatives, and MSG. The newer varieties no longer have these additives, and the savings can be rather astonishing. A quart of free-range, gluten-free chicken broth can cost as much as $3.50. A jar of Superior Touch Brand's Better Than Bouillon runs $6 for 16 ounces, and makes 16 quarts of broth. That's an enormous price difference!

Time is a premium commodity in most busy households, and you will quickly discover that you not only save money by utilizing your slow cooker, you save valuable time as well. One way in which I save time in the kitchen is to brown a lot of ground meat (usually turkey or beef) at a time. If I'm already pulling the skillet out to brown a pound of meat for a particular recipe, I'll brown a few more pounds to store in the freezer for future use. I also choose to chop my onions all at once in the food processor. I despise chopping onions, and instead dice a whole 5-pound bag of onions at one time, and freeze in 1-cup serving sizes in ziplock freezer bags. When an onion is needed in a recipe, I pull out my frozen bag and let it float in a bowl of hot water until thawed—this saves so much time (and tears!) on a busy morning.

I also prefer to buy bags of baby carrots to toss into the slow cooker instead of peeling and chopping large carrots. I've found that the price difference isn't enough to persuade me to pull out the cutting board and peeler.

I try to keep the following pantry and freezer staples on hand in our home kitchen:

A-1® steak sauce
all-purpose flour (I use Pamela's Baking Mix as my gluten-free all-purpose flour)
beans (dried and canned)

broth

brown and white rice (long grain and instant)

butter

canned fruit (peaches, pears, mandarin oranges)

canned tomatoes

cheese (shredded and block, lots of varieties depending on sales)

chicken thighs and breast pieces

cornstarch

cottage cheese

cream (heavy, half-and-half)

cream cheese

eggs

fresh fruit: apples, bananas, oranges, berries

fresh vegetables: potatoes, onions, carrots, celery, bell peppers

frozen vegetables

ground beef and turkey

ketchup

milk

mustard

oatmeal (rolled, steel-cut, ours is certified gluten-free)

orange juice

pasta, all shapes and sizes (brown rice pasta for us!)

soy sauce (gluten-free)

sugar (white and brown)

vinegar (apple cider, red wine, balsamic, white wine)

wine (white and red, the mini airplane bottles for cooking)

Worcestershire sauce (gluten-free)

yogurt

Another way to save money on meals is to travel with your slow cooker. When on vacation, I regularly seek out hotel or vacation rentals that include a small kitchenette. Instead of using the pots and pans the rental provides, I bring along my own slow cooker and load it up in the morning before we head out sightseeing. My children are well behaved, but after a long day out, they rarely want to put on "restaurant manners." It's nice to know that we can come back to the room and enjoy a fully cooked meal without waiting in line or spending gobs of additional money.

Choosing a Slow Cooker

Your basic slow cooker has a cooking element (which is the part with the cord) and removable stoneware into which you load the food. Some of the older slow cooker models don't have this removable section, but all of the new ones on the market do.

Please refer to your owner's manual for the proper use and care of your slow cooker. When slow cooking, the cooking time is a range—if you know that your particular slow cooker seems to cook fast, stick to the low end of the cooking time. When preparing delicate dishes and when baking, keep an eye on your cooker and don't venture too far away.

I would highly recommend purchasing a programmable slow cooker. This type of slow cooker has either buttons or a knob that lets the home cook decide on the cooking temperature (high or low), and can be set to cook in thirty-minute intervals ranging from one to twenty hours. When the set cooking time has elapsed, the machine automatically switches to a warm setting, keeping your food hot and ready to serve when you arrive home at the end of a busy day. When using this type of slow cooker, opt to set it for the lower end of the suggested cooking time. If you're out of the house for 10 hours and the suggested cooking range is for between 6 and 8 hours, set it for 6 and let the cooker stay on warm until you arrive home. If your meat and potatoes aren't quite bite tender, you can always flip it to high while you change clothes and set the table. You can pick up a good programmable slow cooker for under $100.

I recommend keeping your pot two-thirds to three-quarters full for optimum performance. Although there are many different sizes of slow cookers on the market, you do not need to go out and buy them all. If you are going to purchase one, and one only, opt for a 6-quart. You can still make all the appetizers, dips, and fondues in this one machine by simply inserting an oven-safe dish (Corningware®, Pyrex®) into your removable stoneware to create a smaller cooking vessel.

ℛeal Life

I love how the slow cooker allows me to have wiggle room when preparing meals. Before I began my Year of Slow Cooking challenge, I was uncertain which spices go together and why. I have certainly expanded my culinary expertise during the past few years, but I would never consider myself to be a great traditional cook. I like having fun. I treat the slow cooker as an Easy-Bake™ oven for grown-ups.

I love the fact that I can put something on and wander away without fearing the food will burn to a crisp or boil over (things that happen often when I cook using traditional methods). I also like the fact that I can taste and tweak spices while cooking with plenty of time to "fix" anything that might happen. I've been known to accidentally add a tablespoon of salt instead of a teaspoon. The low and steady heat of the slow cooker gives me the opportunity to scoop out my mistake without burning my fingers, or the time needed to add more broth or ingredients to balance out my flub.

Cooking should be fun. When preparing dinner becomes a chore and it's no longer enjoyable, money is wasted ordering pizza or takeout. One of the reasons the slow cooker has become such an invaluable tool in our house is because I can make do with pantry staples or meat I buy on clearance. Some of our favorite meals have occurred when I just started opening cabinets and dumping stuff in the pot. I urge you to do the same. Play. You might just surprise yourself with what you come up with!

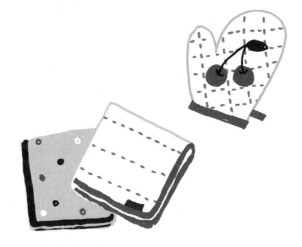

$7
and
Under

The recipes in this section have all been made for a total not exceeding $7. Many of the dishes are actually right around the $5 mark and feed a family of four. This section houses most of the vegetarian main courses that appear in this book. Cutting back on meat consumption will *always* save you money. One of the most expensive bean recipes shared in this cookbook (Potluck Beans, page 230) can be made quite cheaply by simply omitting the meat.

Most of the soups listed can be made meat-free without compromising taste, for additional savings. You can "beef up" a meatless soup or stew by adding dried or canned beans or a pound of cubed tofu for an extra bit of protein and fiber. It's not worth it to skimp on portion size or taste in order to save money. All that leads to is frustration, and leaves you rummaging through the kitchen cupboards an hour after mealtime because you're still hungry.

Many Americans overindulge in portion size and meat consumption. It's recommended to not eat more than a deck-of-cards–size piece of meat in one sitting. If you find that you consistently serve a larger portion for your main course, you'll notice immediate grocery store savings by sticking to this smaller amount. I usually allot a half pound of meat per person when I cook, and this amount provides enough leftovers (I'm serving two adults, and two small children so far—your mileage may vary!) that I can stretch for lunch the next day, or repurpose into a soup or casserole. Many of my meals serve six people or more, just so I can plan ahead and not cook daily!

I've received many letters and e-mails from frustrated wives who complain that their husbands only want to eat large portions of meat and potatoes for dinner. I feel your pain, and I'm sorry. My suggestion is to go slowly and don't try to make too many changes all at once. Begin adding more vegetables and beans to your main dishes, and slowly trim the meat until you're cooking no more than one half pound per person. Your wallet, your waistline, and your heart will thank you—and so will his!

BEVERAGES

Caramel Apple Spiced Cider   16

Irish Coffee   17

Luncheon Lemonade   18

CARAMEL APPLE SPICED CIDER

serves 4

The Ingredients

    4 cups apple cider
    3 tablespoons caramel syrup (the ice cream topping)
    $1/2$ tablespoon ground cinnamon
    $1/4$ teaspoon ground cloves
    4 tablespoons sweetened whipped cream (optional)

The Directions

Use a 2-quart slow cooker. Pour the apple cider into the slow cooker and add the caramel syrup. Add the spices. Cover and cook on low for 4 hours, high for 2, or until heated throughout. Stir well and ladle into mugs with a squirt of whipped cream, if you'd like (I do!).

The Verdict

Last winter, my children tasted a sample of this drink at our local coffee house. When I learned what the outlet was charging for an extra-small–size drink, I decided to make a batch at home. The kids were thrilled with my creation and declared me "the best mom ever"—a title I proudly wore for approximately 10 minutes, which was about how long it took for me to notice there was caramel sauce ground into the couch cushions.

IRISH COFFEE

serves 4

The Ingredients

3 cups strong black coffee
¼ cup Bailey's Irish Cream (more if you're feeling feisty!)
⅓ cup heavy whipping cream
1 tablespoon cocoa powder
4 tablespoons sweetened whipped cream

The Directions

Use a 2-quart slow cooker. Combine the coffee and Irish Cream in your slow cooker. Stir in the whipping cream and cocoa powder. Cover and cook on low for 3 hours, or on high for about 90 minutes. Serve in mugs with a dollop of sweetened whipped cream (the stuff in the can!).

The Verdict

My friend Georgia and I made these on a rainy day, and enjoyed them a lot. The sweetened whipped cream is important, as the coffee and Irish Cream are quite strong in flavor without this touch of sugar.

LUNCHEON LEMONADE
serves 10

The Ingredients
4 cups water
1 cup orange juice
2 (12-ounce) cans pineapple juice
½ cup sugar
½ teaspoon whole cloves
1 cinnamon stick
1 lemon, sliced in rings

The Directions
Use a 4-quart slow cooker. Pour the water and juices into your cooker. Stir in the sugar. Add the whole cloves and the cinnamon stick. Float the lemon slices on top. Cover and cook on low for 3 to 4 hours, or until heated through. To serve guests, provide a ladle, leave the lid off, and turn the slow cooker to low. Your drink will not stay hot enough if left on the warm setting.

The Verdict
This is a light, citrusy punch that's perfect to serve at a brunch, shower, or springtime party. It's not overpowering, and pairs really well with finger food. The smell of simmering cinnamon and cloves is such an inviting fragrance. Your house could be a disaster zone, but your guests will only remember the lovely homey smell.

BREAKFASTS

Leftovers for Breakfast   20

Multigrain Porridge   21

Steel Cut Oatmeal   22

LEFTOVERS FOR BREAKFAST

serves 8

The Ingredients

1 (30-ounce) bag frozen hash brown potatoes
2 cups diced cooked meat (I've used chicken, beef, corned beef, ham, and a combination—it's all good)
2 cups diced cooked vegetables (broccoli, peppers, carrots, or the like)
8 eggs
1 cup milk
2 cups shredded cheese (your choice!)
salt and pepper to taste at the table

The Directions

Use a 6-quart slow cooker. Put the frozen hash browns into your slow cooker. In a large mixing bowl, whisk together the meat, vegetables, eggs, milk, and cheese. Pour the mixture on top of the potatoes. Cover and cook on low for 7 hours, or on high for 3 to 4 hours.

The Verdict

This is so easy to throw together, and uses up the contents from all those little Tupperwares floating around at the back of the fridge by the end of the week. I like to make this casserole after family holidays like St. Patrick's Day and Thanksgiving. Even though the main leftover ingredients (corned beef and turkey) taste completely different, the casseroles always turn out excellent.

MULTIGRAIN PORRIDGE
serves 10

The Ingredients
2 tablespoons butter
3/4 cup brown rice
1/4 cup quinoa
1 cup rolled oats (I use gluten-free certified oats)
1 cup steel cut oats (I use gluten-free certified oats)
2 Granny Smith apples, cored and diced (I didn't peel)
2 teaspoons vanilla extract
2 teaspoons ground cinnamon
1/4 to 1/3 cup brown sugar (start with the smaller amount and add more to taste)
10 cups water

The Directions
Use a 6-quart slow cooker. Butter the inside of your stoneware insert. Rinse the brown rice and quinoa thoroughly in cool running water, and dump into the buttered crock. Add both kinds of oats, the diced apples, vanilla, cinnamon, and brown sugar. Pour in all 10 cups of water. Cover and cook on low for 6 hours, on high for about 4, or until the brown rice is completely tender. Take the lid off of your cooker and stir very well. Unplug, and let the porridge sit in the cooling slow cooker for 10 to 15 minutes before serving. Add additional brown sugar, if desired, to taste at the table.

The Verdict
This is a great breakfast to energize your day. Quinoa, steel cut oats, and brown rice have all been deemed "super foods," and are packed with fiber and nutrients. I can find certified gluten-free oats at Whole Foods, and I also buy them in bulk through Amazon.com. Even when purchasing the higher-priced gluten-free ingredients, this breakfast works out to well under $1 a serving. The leftovers freeze and reheat beautifully.

STEEL CUT OATMEAL

serves 4

The Ingredients

1 cup steel cut oats (mine were certified gluten-free)
4 cups water
¼ cup milk, plus more for serving
3 tablespoons brown sugar
1 teaspoon vanilla extract
1 teaspoon ground cinnamon
butter to grease pan
diced fresh fruit (optional)

The Directions

Use a 6-quart slow cooker and an inserted 9×5×3-inch loaf pan. In a mixing bowl, combine the oats, water, milk, sugar, vanilla, and cinnamon. Pour the oat mixture into a buttered loaf pan. Place the loaf pan into your slow cooker, and add water around the base of the loaf pan until it reaches halfway up the sides of the pan, taking care not to slosh water into your oatmeal.

Cover and cook on low for 7 to 9 hours, or until the oatmeal has set. Spoon into serving dishes, and add diced fresh fruit and additional milk, if desired.

The Verdict

This is a very basic steel cut oats recipe, and I love that it can cook overnight. Steel cut oats, a fantastic source of whole grain soluble fiber, are a great way to start a busy day. It's hard to believe how soft and tender these oats become since the raw pieces are so coarse and gravel-like.

APPETIZERS

Baked Herbed Feta   24

Grape Jelly and Chili Sauce Little Smokies   25

Ranch Party Mix   26

Taco Dip   27

Thyme for Goat Cheese   29

BAKED HERBED FETA

serves 4

The Ingredients

1 (8-ounce) slab feta cheese
¼ teaspoon crushed red pepper flakes
¼ teaspoon dried oregano
1 tablespoon extra-virgin olive oil
1 tablespoon lemon juice
crusty bread or crackers for dipping (I make crostini from a loaf of brown rice bread, see below)

The Directions

Use a 2-quart slow cooker. Unwrap the cheese and place in the center of your stoneware insert. Sprinkle the red pepper flakes and oregano on top. Drizzle on the olive oil and lemon juice evenly. Cover and cook on low for 2 to 3 hours, or until the cheese is quite soft but still in block form. Serve right out of the crock, with a butter knife to spread onto crackers or crostini.

To make gluten-free crostini: I use a loaf of Food for Life® brown rice bread. Cut the bread into 1-inch-wide strips. Brush olive oil onto each side, and sprinkle with kosher salt and freshly ground black pepper. Bake on a cookie sheet at 400° for 12 to 15 minutes, or until the bread is fully toasted. Flip once during cooking.

The Verdict

Just when I thought I couldn't possibly enjoy feta any more than I already do, I tried this. *Oh, yum!* We served this to our friends Jennifer and Adam and ate so much we forgot to order dinner. The kids (ages one, three, five, and eight) all liked it too!

GRAPE JELLY AND CHILI SAUCE
LITTLE SMOKIES

serves 8

The Ingredients

1 pound Little Smokies sausage

1 (12-ounce) bottle chili sauce (housed near the ketchup)

1 (18-ounce) jar grape jelly

The Directions

Use a 4-quart slow cooker. Put the Little Smokies into the slow cooker. Pour in the chili sauce and grape jelly. Stir to combine. Cover and cook on low for 4 hours, on high for 2, or until heated throughout. Serve with toothpicks right out of the slow cooker.

The Verdict

This is our family's favorite Little Smokies recipe, and it's the easiest. Kids and adults both like the flavor combination, strange as it sounds.

RANCH PARTY MIX

serves 12

The Ingredients
   9 cups Chex® cereal (Rice and Corn Chex® are gluten-free)
   2 cups pretzel sticks (I use Glutino® brand)
   1 cup salted peanuts
   1 (1-ounce) package ranch salad-dressing mix (see page 56 to make your own mix)
   ½ cup powdered Parmesan cheese
   ¼ cup butter, melted

The Directions
Use a 6-quart slow cooker. Put the cereal into the slow cooker, and add the pretzels and peanuts. Sprinkle on the dried ranch mix and the Parmesan cheese. Add the melted butter, and toss the cereal mixture with two large spoons to coat. Cover and cook on high for 2 hours, stirring every 20 minutes or so. The cereal on the outside edges will burn if you don't stir (actually, I kind of like the burnt pieces), but the wiggle-room with this recipe is much greater than if using the oven to cook.

The Verdict
We are a Chex® party mix family. I keep two to three boxes of cereal on hand to munch on and for snack mixes. It makes a great after-school snack, and the smell while cooking is warm and comforting. I'm thrilled that these cereals are now clearly labeled gluten-free and I can find them everywhere.

TACO DIP

serves 12

The Ingredients

1 (8-ounce) block cream cheese
1 pound Velveeta®
2 cups bottled salsa (I like Southwest style with beans and corn)
1 (1.25-ounce) envelope taco seasoning mix (McCormick is gluten-free, or make your own, recipe below)

The Directions

Use a 4-quart or larger slow cooker. Dump everything in. It will not look pretty, and that's okay. Cover and cook on low for about 3 hours, on high for 90 minutes, or until the cheeses have fully melted and are heated through. Stir well and serve with your favorite tortilla chips.

Or celery, if you must . . .

HOMEMADE TACO SEASONING MIX

2 teaspoons instant minced onion
1 teaspoon chili powder
$\frac{1}{2}$ teaspoon cornstarch
$\frac{1}{2}$ teaspoon crushed dried red pepper
$\frac{1}{2}$ teaspoon instant minced garlic
$\frac{1}{4}$ teaspoon dried oregano
$\frac{1}{2}$ teaspoon ground cumin

Mix all ingredients together. This recipe equals one packet of purchased taco seasoning.

(CONTINUED)

The Verdict

I made this dip for a party, and the adults pretty much fought the kids to get their fill—which is saying a lot, because the oldest kid was nine, and I *know* for a fact there was plenty of double-dipping going on.

I saw one of our neighbors use his finger to scrape out the bowl. I didn't tell him I was watching.

THYME FOR GOAT CHEESE

serves 4 to 6

The Ingredients
1 (11-ounce) package fresh goat cheese
2$\frac{1}{2}$ teaspoons finely chopped fresh thyme leaves, plus an additional sprig or two for garnish
1 tablespoon extra-virgin olive oil
$\frac{1}{2}$ teaspoon freshly ground black pepper
crackers or bread cubes for serving (see page 24 for crostini)

The Directions
Use a 2-quart slow cooker. If desired, place an oven-safe ramekin that you'd like to use for serving into the bottom of your slow cooker, and place the goat cheese inside. Otherwise, simply place the cheese directly into the bottom of your slow cooker insert. Press the thyme leaves into the top of the cheese. Drizzle the olive oil on top and add the black pepper. Cover and cook on low for 2 to 3 hours, or until the cheese has softened and become easy to spread. Lift the inserted dish out of the slow cooker, and serve at the table with crackers or bread cubes.

The Verdict
This is such a simple appetizer, but sometimes simplicity pays off in a big way.

SOUPS & STEWS

Baked Potato Soup *31*

Creamy Tomato Soup *32*

End of Summer Harvest Soup *33*

Lentil Soup *35*

Old-Fashioned Chicken Noodle Soup *36*

Sauerkraut Soup *38*

Smoky Bean and Corn Soup *39*

Zesty Burger Soup *40*

BAKED POTATO SOUP

serves 10

The Ingredients

    5 pounds potatoes, peeled and diced in 1- to 2-inch chunks
    1 small onion, diced
    4 garlic cloves, minced
    1 teaspoon seasoned salt
    $1/2$ teaspoon black pepper
    $1/2$ teaspoon cayenne pepper
    2 quarts chicken broth
    2 (8-ounce) packages cream cheese (to add at the end)
    crumbled bacon, green onion, or chives as garnish (optional)

The Directions

Use a 6-quart slow cooker. Put the potatoes into your stoneware, and add the onion and garlic. Sprinkle in the seasonings and pour in the chicken broth. Cover and cook on low for 8 hours, or on high for 4. The potatoes should be fork-tender. You can use a potato masher or a handheld stick blender to mash the potatoes into the soup. You want to get rid of all large chunks of potato to make a smooth soup.

After smashing the potatoes, squeeze in both packages of cream cheese and replace the lid of your cooker. Cook on high for about 30 minutes, or until the cream cheese is completely dissolved. Stir a few times during this 30 minutes.

Garnish with crumbled bacon, green onion, or chives.

The Verdict

This is a fantastic soup, and my family thought that the bacon on top really sealed the deal. My kids both ate a bowl when it was first finished around 4:00 PM, and another later in the evening. Thank you to my Web site readers Jennifer, Jenny, Jenny Y., Julie, and Charlotte for this wonderful and hearty soup recipe suggestion.

CREAMY TOMATO SOUP

serves 4 to 6

The Ingredients

2 (14-ounce) cans crushed tomatoes
1 yellow onion, peeled and chopped
1 cup beef broth
¼ cup brown sugar
2 teaspoons dried basil
1 tablespoon gluten-free Worcestershire sauce
1 teaspoon unsweetened cocoa powder (the secret ingredient!)
1 (14-ounce) can evaporated milk (to add later)
2 tablespoons butter (to add later)

The Directions

Use a 4-quart slow cooker. In a blender or food processor, puree the tomatoes and onion. Pour the mixture into your slow cooker, and add the broth, brown sugar, basil, Worcestershire sauce, and cocoa powder. Stir. Cover and cook on low for 6 hours, or on high for 3 to 4. Stir in the milk and plop in the butter. Cover and cook on high for 15 minutes, or until the butter melts and the soup is hot.

The Verdict

I am not a tomato soup eater. I don't like the stuff in the can, and I won't order it in a restaurant because I'm worried it will taste like the stuff in a can. This doesn't, I promise. This tomato soup is rich, creamy, and silky, and I licked my bowl clean. My parents liked it, too!

END OF SUMMER HARVEST SOUP

serves 8

The Ingredients

4 zucchini, washed well and sliced in ¼-inch rounds

2 yellow summer squash, washed well and sliced in ¼-inch rounds

1 medium yellow onion, diced

2 cups cherry tomatoes, halved or quartered (depending on size)

⅓ cup dry white cannellini beans (this doesn't sound like a lot, but they swell!)

4 cups chicken broth

1 cup prepared pasta sauce

1 cup water

1 tablespoon Italian seasoning

½ cup pasta (to add 20 minutes before serving)

salt and pepper to taste

Grated Parmesan and Romano cheeses as garnish (optional)

The Directions

Use a 6-quart slow cooker. Place the sliced squash into the slow cooker, with the diced onion and tomatoes. Rinse your beans in hot water and add to the cooker. Add the broth, pasta sauce, and water. Stir in the Italian seasoning.

Cover and cook on low for 8 to 10 hours, or until the beans have reached the desired tenderness. Stir in the raw pasta 20 minutes before serving. Ladle into bowls and serve with grated Parmesan and Romano cheeses, if desired.

(CONTINUED)

The Verdict

What a gorgeous and delicious soup! I was motivated to make this soup with garden vegetables after reading Barbara Kingsolver's fantastic memoir, *Animal, Vegetable, Miracle.* I loved how the tomatoes burst completely while slow cooked, and how the squash practically disappeared, so there was no need to chew it—the squash provides an awesome texture and flavor, and since it turns translucent, my kids ate it without fuss. I liked how the prepared pasta sauce gave the broth an *oomph* sometimes missing in homemade soups and provided a rich color.

LENTIL SOUP

serves 6

The Ingredients
1 pound lentils
1 (14.5-ounce) can diced tomatoes
2 small onions, peeled and diced
5 garlic cloves, diced
2 tablespoons apple cider vinegar
1/2 teaspoon sugar
1 teaspoon dried oregano
1/2 teaspoon kosher salt
1/2 teaspoon pepper
4 cups water

The Directions
Use a 6-quart slow cooker. Rinse the lentils well in hot water. Put into the bottom of your slow cooker with the entire can of tomatoes. Add the onions, garlic, apple cider vinegar, sugar, and spices. Pour in the water. Cover and cook on low for 8 hours, or on high for 4 to 5 hours. Add a bit more salt to taste at the table.

The Verdict
This is a filling and comforting lentil soup, without the canned metallic taste. Lentils are uber-healthy, and are a super-inexpensive staple to keep in your pantry. My girls ate their portions, although it took a bit of persuasion to get them to try what they thought looked like "bowls of mud." I added a bit more salt to my serving, and Adam added a shake of Tabasco sauce.

OLD-FASHIONED CHICKEN NOODLE SOUP

serves 6

The Ingredients

6 cups water

1½ cups diced cooked chicken

1 medium sweet potato, peeled and chunked

1 cup broccoli florets

1 small onion, diced

2 teaspoons chicken bouillon granules (check for gluten!)

1 tablespoon plus 1 teaspoon balsamic vinegar

kosher salt to taste (probably a good teaspoon, since the base is water)

50-cent-piece size or so handful of raw spaghetti noodles to add at the end (I used Trader Joe's brown rice spaghetti)

1 large handful raw spinach leaves to add at the end

Grated Parmesan and Asiago cheeses as garnish (optional)

The Directions

Use a 6-quart slow cooker. Pour 6 cups of water into your slow cooker and add the chicken. Add the potato, broccoli, and onion. Stir in the bouillon and vinegar. Salt to taste. Cover and cook on low for 6 to 8 hours, or until the sweet potato is tender and the onion is translucent.

Fifteen minutes before serving, put in the raw spaghetti noodles and a large handful of spinach. Cover and flip to high.

Garnish with Parmesan and Asiago cheeses, if desired.

The Verdict

This is such a wonderful, comforting soup. The balsamic vinegar does two things: 1) It provides a nice color, and 2) it brings the chicken flavor out nicely while leaving a touch of a tang. The tang is nice, because it fools your tongue into thinking it's tasting salt—which is mostly what you taste in canned chicken noodle soups.

My big kids both had thirds! I think my head might have exploded.

SAUERKRAUT SOUP

serves 6

The Ingredients

8 ounces button mushrooms, sliced
1 small onion, peeled and diced
2 tablespoons olive oil
4 cups chicken broth
1 (14.5-ounce) can sauerkraut
1 (14.5-ounce) can crushed Italian-style tomatoes
$\frac{1}{2}$ teaspoon caraway seeds
1 celery stalk, chopped
1 carrot, peeled and chopped

The Directions

Use a 4-quart slow cooker. In a skillet on the stove, brown the mushrooms and onion in the olive oil. When lightly browned, put them into your slow cooker. Add the broth and the entire cans of sauerkraut and tomatoes. Stir in the caraway, celery, and carrot. Cover and cook on low for 6 to 8 hours. Serve with crusty bread.

The Verdict

I *do* like sauerkraut! I'm annoyed at myself for avoiding it for so long—I don't know why I was so hesitant to give it a try. A great big thank-you to Rosalind for sending me this recipe. Taking the time to brown the mushrooms and onion in the olive oil is an important step as it provides a bit of fat from the olive oil and lots of flavor.

SMOKY BEAN AND CORN SOUP

serves 6

The Ingredients

1 (20-ounce) package bean soup mix, soaked overnight
1 tablespoon dried minced onion flakes or 1 medium onion, finely diced
1 (15-ounce) can corn (and juice)
4 cups chicken broth
1 ham hock with leftover meat, or ½ pound raw bacon, diced

The Directions

Use a 6-quart slow cooker. Sort through the beans, and pick out any that are broken or shriveled. If your bean mix came with a flavor packet, toss it out. Soak the beans overnight in enough water to cover by 3 inches, or boil rapidly on the stove for 10 minutes, then let sit, covered, in the hot water for 1 hour.

Put the beans into the slow cooker. Add the onion and corn. Pour in the chicken broth, and add the ham hock or diced bacon. Cover and cook on low for 8 to 10 hours, or until the beans have softened completely and begun to split. Remove the ham hock and cut off any remaining meat. Stir this meat into your soup.

The Verdict

What a wonderful soup to come home to on a rainy day! The beans and corn pair with the ham or bacon to create a lovely, filling, balanced meal. I like to serve my soup with a loaf of homemade cornbread (I use a gluten-free mix).

ZESTY BURGER SOUP

serves 6

The Ingredients

1 pound lean ground beef, browned and drained
2 (10.5-ounce) cans tomatoes and chiles, drained (Rotel)
1 (15-ounce) can whole kernel corn, undrained
1 (15-ounce) can black beans, drained and rinsed
4 cups chicken broth
shredded sharp cheddar cheese (optional)

The Directions

Use a 6-quart slow cooker. Brown the meat in a skillet on the stovetop and drain the fat. Combine the meat, canned tomatoes, corn, and beans. Pour in the chicken broth. Cover and cook on low for 6 to 8 hours, or until fully hot and the flavors have melded. Serve with shredded cheddar cheese, if desired.

The Verdict

We all really liked this soup. The hamburger fills you up quickly, and the leftovers can be stretched into a taco or burrito filling for an additional meal. This is a filling comfort soup to come home to on a cold fall evening. The flavor is similar to a mild chili, and my kids enjoy sprinkling cheddar cheese onto their servings at the table.

BEANS

Baked Bean Soup   42

Black Beans with Cilantro   44

Coconut Red Beans and Rice   45

Calico Bean Soup   47

Cowboy Beans   49

Hoppin' John   51

Poor Man's Chili   52

Vegetarian Baked Beans   53

BAKED BEAN SOUP

serves 6

The Ingredients

1 (15-ounce) can white kidney beans or pinto beans, undrained (if you are going to use dry beans, presoak ⅔ cup overnight, and then cook until the beans are soft)
1 cup finely diced onion
1 cup diced carrot
3 teaspoons prepared Dijon mustard
2 tablespoons unsulfured molasses
1 tablespoon gluten-free soy sauce
2 teaspoons apple cider vinegar
1 tablespoon chili powder
1 (14.5-ounce) can fire-roasted tomatoes (and the juice!)
2 cups water
salt to taste

The Directions

Use a 6-quart slow cooker. Put the beans into the cooker, and top with the onion and carrot. Add all the seasonings and spices. Pour in the entire can of tomatoes, add the water, and stir.

Cover and cook on low for 7 to 8 hours, or on high for 4 to 5 hours. If your beans were dry, you might need to go as long as 10 hours, depending on the altitude and humidity.

Before serving, pulse a bit with a handheld stick blender to blend some of the beans. This will thicken your broth and provide a richer flavor. If you don't have a stick blender, scoop out about 1 cup of liquid, pulse carefully in a traditional blender, and stir back into the cooker. Add salt to taste.

The Verdict

I love this soup. It tastes just like you'd imagine a can of blended pork and beans would taste, except better. There's a slight kick from the chili powder, but it's not overpowering. If you're serving super young children or adults who don't like spicy food, reduce the chili powder to $1/2$ tablespoon and use only $1/2$ cup of diced onion. You can certainly add bacon or sausage, but it tastes fantastic all on its own.

BLACK BEANS WITH CILANTRO

serves 8

The Ingredients

1 pound dry black beans, sorted and soaked overnight

6 cups chicken broth

2 tablespoons dried cilantro

1 tablespoon garlic powder

1 cup chopped fresh cilantro (to add after cooking)

The Directions

Use a 6-quart slow cooker. Sort the beans and soak them overnight in a bunch of water (they should be covered by at least two inches of water). In the morning, drain the water and pour the beans into an empty slow cooker. Add the chicken broth, dried cilantro, and garlic powder. Stir well to combine. Cover and cook on low for 8 to 12 hours, or until the beans are bite-tender. If you live in a high altitude, you will need to cook them longer.

Toss the hot cooked beans with chopped cilantro before serving.

The Verdict

This is my favorite way to have black beans. I like to cook a big batch on the weekends, and then use the cooked beans in salads or on top of rice for lunch. My children like to munch on cold black beans with their fingers for a snack, although they pick out all of the "green stuff." The seasoned flavor from the cilantro and garlic is perfect without needing salt. This recipe comes from Kalyn Denny, who writes fantastic South Beach Diet–friendly recipes at kalynskitchen.blogspot.com.

COCONUT RED BEANS AND RICE

serves 8

The Ingredients

1 cup dry small red beans (soaked overnight, and then boiled for 10 minutes)
1 large onion, finely diced
2 garlic cloves, minced
1 teaspoon crushed red pepper flakes
1 (14-ounce) can coconut milk
3 cups chicken broth
1 1/2 cups long-grain basmati white rice
1/2 teaspoon kosher salt
2 limes, cut in wedges, for serving (optional)

The Directions

Use a 4-quart slow cooker. Sort the beans and soak them overnight in a bunch of water (they should be covered by at least two inches of water). In the morning, drain the water and add the beans to a pot of fresh water. Boil rapidly on the stove for 10 minutes. Red beans must be boiled before adding to the slow cooker to kill any possible toxins that occur naturally. Drain and rinse the beans, and drop them into an empty slow cooker. Add the onion, garlic, and red pepper flakes. Pour in the coconut milk and chicken broth. Stir in the raw rice and kosher salt. Cover and cook on low for 8 to 10 hours, or until the beans are bite-tender. Before eating, squeeze a bit of lime juice over the top for a great tropical citrus flavor.

(CONTINUED)

The Verdict

I really liked how this tasted, and loved how the beans and rice cooked together in one pot. My grandma took home a large Tupperware of leftovers, and reported back that the beans and rice froze and reheated beautifully. I used full-fat coconut milk. I greatly prefer the flavor of the full-fat stuff to the lighter version. If you're uncomfortable using this variety, you can add a drop of coconut extract to the ingredients before cooking to intensify the coconut flavor.

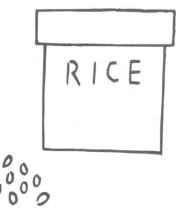

CALICO BEAN SOUP

serves 10 easily

The Ingredients

1 pound assorted dry beans (I used small red [see Note], lima, Great Northern, black-eyed peas, split peas, and pinto)

3 tablespoons dried minced onion flakes

1 tablespoon dried parsley

1 tablespoon garlic powder

1 tablespoon celery seed (or chop up a bunch of celery if you already have it in the house)

1 teaspoon seasoned salt

1 teaspoon paprika

1 teaspoon sugar

1/2 teaspoon black pepper

2 cans (25 to 30 ounces) diced tomatoes (whatever you have on hand—flavored, Rotel, etc.)

4 cups broth

4 cups water

The Directions

Use a 6-quart slow cooker. Soak your beans overnight in enough water to cover completely with another 3 inches or so. Drain well and add to the pot. If you don't have time to soak the beans for hours and hours, put them in a large stockpot with a bunch of water and bring to a boil. Boil rapidly for 10 minutes, then turn off the heat and cover the pot. Let your beans sit for an hour, then drain and use.

Note: If you opt to use any red beans in your soup, you must boil them rapidly on the stovetop for at least 10 minutes to kill a possible toxin that occurs naturally in red beans.

(CONTINUED)

After the beans are in the slow cooker, add all the spices and canned tomatoes. Pour in the broth and water. Cover and cook on low for 10 to 20 hours, or until the beans have begun to split and thicken the broth. You can also remove about a cup of beans and blend them, then stir back in to thicken the broth nicely (or do a few pulses with a hand mixer!).

The Verdict

I make this soup when I need to clean the pantry from all the mostly empty bags of dry beans that collect over a few months. The last time I made it, I put the soup on during the day and fell asleep on the couch in the evening while it was cooking (we had a new baby in the house). When Adam tried to wake me at 11:15 PM to remind me that the soup was still on, I muttered, "It's beans. they could cook forever, it's fine." And I was right! This soup cooked on low for 19 hours. It's delicious, and can certainly be completely vegetarian if you don't use liquefied chicken for broth the way I did.

COWBOY BEANS

serves 6 to 8

The Ingredients

    1 pound dry pinto beans, soaked overnight
    1 pound lean ground beef or turkey (optional)
    1 small yellow onion, diced
    1 red bell pepper, seeded and chopped
    1 to 2 tablespoons gluten-free Worcestershire sauce
    2 tablespoons chili powder
    2 teaspoons kosher salt
    1 teaspoon dry mustard
    $\frac{1}{2}$ teaspoon black pepper
    1 (10-ounce) can tomatoes and chiles (Rotel)
    1 to 2 tablespoons apple cider vinegar
    7 cups water
    sliced jalapeños (optional)

The Directions

Sort the pinto beans and soak overnight in lots of fresh water. If you live in a climate where the house gets terribly hot overnight, put the beans in the refrigerator to soak to keep icky bacteria from accumulating. In the morning, drain your beans and pick out any that have split open, or look discolored and shriveled.

Pour the beans into a 6-quart slow cooker. Brown the beef or turkey, if using, and onion and pepper on the stove, and drain well. While the meat is cooking, add the rest of the ingredients into your slow cooker. Start with 1 tablespoon each of Worcestershire sauce and apple cider vinegar. Add the meat, top with 7 cups water, and stir to combine. Cover and cook on low for 8 to 10 hours, or on high

(CONTINUED)

for about 6. My beans took 6 hours on high to tenderize, and then they sat on warm for another 3 hours. We're at sea level. If you live in a higher altitude, your beans will take longer to soften.

Taste the beans. If you'd like your beans to have more of a twang, add some more Worcestershire sauce and apple cider vinegar. Top with sliced jalapeños, if desired.

The Verdict

Even though summer is prime grilling time, I really like to plug in the slow cooker for hassle-free side dishes on the nights we decide to grill. The difference between Cowboy Beans and a traditional chili is the twangy flavor that comes from the Worcestershire sauce and apple cider vinegar. The more you add, the twangier it becomes.

HOPPIN' JOHN

serves 10

The Ingredients

1 pound dry black-eyed peas, soaked overnight
4 cups chicken broth
1 pound smoked sausage, sliced
1/2 cup instant rice
1 (10.5-ounce) can tomatoes and chiles (Rotel)
1 bunch collard greens or kale, chopped
1/2 teaspoon kosher salt
1/4 teaspoon black pepper

The Directions

Use a 6-quart slow cooker. Sort the beans and soak overnight in lots of water. If you don't have time to soak them overnight, you can boil them rapidly on the stovetop for 10 minutes, then let the beans sit, covered, in the hot water for 1 hour before draining and using in the slow cooker.

Put the beans into your slow cooker. Add the broth and sliced sausage. Stir in the rice and the tomatoes and chiles. Add the greens, and sprinkle on the salt and pepper. You may need to shove the greens in with a wooden spoon to get them to fit inside the pot.

Cover and cook on low for 8 to 12 hours, or until beans are soft and tender. Stir well before serving.

The Verdict

Hoppin' John is traditionally eaten on New Year's Day to bring good luck and prosperity throughout the year. This is a fantastic recipe—the beans have a great smoky flavor from the sausage, and the greens wilt and take on this flavor as well. I shared these beans (it's really more like a casserole with the rice and sausage) with my grandma, parents, and my brother and sister-in-law (this recipe makes a lot!), and everyone agreed that they were quite tasty.

POOR MAN'S CHILI

serves 6

The Ingredients

1 (15-ounce) can black beans, drained
1 (15-ounce) can garbanzo beans, drained
1 (15-ounce) can kidney beans, drained
1 (15-ounce) can corn, drained
1 cup baby tomatoes (they pop after slow cooking!)
1 (24-ounce) jar prepared pasta sauce
1 teaspoon ground cumin
1 teaspoon ground coriander
1 teaspoon turmeric (not really a "poor" spice, it's a substitute for saffron, but I had it in the cupboard. If you don't have any, you can try a mixture of curry and cardamom, or just omit it altogether)
1 cinnamon stick

The Directions

Use a 6-quart slow cooker. Drain the beans and corn, and put the can contents into your slow cooker. Top with the tomatoes and pasta sauce. Stir in the spices and add a cinnamon stick. Cover and cook on low for 7 to 8 hours, or on high for about 4 hours. If the tomatoes haven't popped on their own, gently poke them with a wooden spoon to pop before serving.

The Verdict

In our house, this is a "free" dinner, because we always happen to have the ingredients on hand. I usually use a handful of baby tomatoes that get squishy in the produce drawer by the end of the week. The cinnamon provides enough of a slightly sweet component to convince the kids that I put brown sugar in their servings. I didn't correct them.

VEGETARIAN BAKED BEANS

serves 8 to 10

The Ingredients

1 pound dry pinto beans
¾ cup ketchup
⅓ cup molasses
1 tablespoon dried minced onion flakes
¼ cup brown sugar
2 teaspoons smoked paprika
1 teaspoon dry mustard

The Directions

Use a 6-quart slow cooker. Sort through the beans and soak overnight. If you don't have time to soak them overnight, boil rapidly on the stovetop for 10 minutes, then remove from the heat and cover. Let the beans sit in hot water for 1 hour before draining and using in the slow cooker.

Put the beans into the cooker, and add the ketchup and molasses. Drop in the onion flakes, brown sugar, smoked paprika, and dry mustard. Stir to distribute the sauces and spices. Cover and cook on low for 8 to 10 hours, high for 4 to 5 hours, or until the beans have softened and are bite-tender.

The Verdict

I am so impressed at how smoky these beans taste without any meat! They are wonderful, and the six of us who tried this recipe didn't miss the meat at all. Smoked paprika is a wonderful spice in vegetarian dishes—I used it in the vegan Sweet Potato Chili, too, on page 231.

SIDE DISHES

Candied Acorn Squash   55

Creamy Ranch Mashed Red Potatoes   56

Irish Potatoes   58

Italian Rice   59

Pineapple Sweet Potatoes   60

Red Potatoes with Rosemary and Garlic   61

Roasted Garlic Spoonbread   62

Roasted Root Vegetables   63

"Scalloped" Potatoes   64

Spaghetti Squash   65

Succotash   66

CANDIED ACORN SQUASH

serves 4

The Ingredients

1 acorn squash
2 apples, peeled, cored, and diced
1 tablespoon butter, melted
2 tablespoons brown sugar
1 tablespoon chopped walnuts
1/2 teaspoon kosher salt
1/2 teaspoon ground cinnamon

The Directions

Use a 4-quart slow cooker. Cut the acorn squash in half. If you have a hard time cutting through the squash, try microwaving it for a minute on high to soften the skin. Scoop out the seeds and discard them. Put the squash into the cooker. In a small mixing bowl, combine the apples, melted butter, brown sugar, walnuts, salt, and cinnamon. Spoon the mixture evenly into the acorn squash halves.

Cover and cook on low for 5 hours, or on high for 2 to 3 hours.

The Verdict

This is my favorite squash recipe, ever. My children love it, and are happy to scoop out the filling from their squash wedge. I think they believe the squash part is just the hard outer skin and they are only really eating the apple/cinnamon/walnut filling, which is totally okay with me. The most difficult part in preparing this side dish is cutting the squash in half. The microwaving trick definitely helps, but please be very careful.

CREAMY RANCH MASHED RED POTATOES

serves 6

The Ingredients

2 pounds red potatoes (I left the skin on, your choice)

1 (8-ounce) package cream cheese

1/2 cup low-fat milk (I used soy)

1 (1-ounce) packet ranch salad dressing mix (Hidden Valley brand does not have gluten, or make your own using the recipe below)

The Directions

Use a 4-quart slow cooker. Wash the potatoes well and cut in quarters. Place all the potatoes into the stoneware insert, and add the block of cream cheese, milk, and the contents of the ranch dressing packet. Cover and cook on low for about 5 hours, or until the potatoes mash easily with a large fork. You can whip the potatoes right in the slow cooker with a hand mixer, or stir well with a large fork to mash into the desired consistency and distribute the cream cheese and ranch flavoring.

HOMEMADE RANCH DIP MIX

makes 1/2 cup

2 teaspoons kosher salt

2 teaspoons dried minced garlic

2 1/2 tablespoons dried minced onion

2 teaspoons freshly ground pepper

2 teaspoons sugar

2 1/2 teaspoons paprika

2 1/2 teaspoons parsley flakes

Combine all the ingredients. Store in an airtight container, and use 1 tablespoon in lieu of packaged ranch mix.

The Verdict

These are wonderful mashed potatoes. I really like how I can cook and mash the potatoes all in one pot, without needing to drain the potatoes or dirty up another bowl. The potatoes are creamy and full of flavor. I liked the rustic look the skins provide (and I hate peeling potatoes), but if you'd like them all one color, you can peel the potatoes before cooking.

IRISH POTATOES
serves 8 to 10

The Ingredients
2$^{1}/_{2}$ pounds potatoes, cut into wedges (I used russet and didn't peel)
$^{1}/_{2}$ cup water
$^{1}/_{2}$ cup butter, melted
1 tablespoon lemon juice
1 tablespoon dried parsley
2 green onions, sliced
3 teaspoons dried dill
$^{1}/_{4}$ teaspoon kosher salt
$^{1}/_{4}$ teaspoon black pepper

The Directions
Use a 6-quart slow cooker. Put the cut potatoes and water into the slow cooker. Cover and cook on low for 5 to 6 hours, or until the potatoes are fork-tender. Drain the accumulated liquid and put the potatoes back into the crock. Add the melted butter and seasonings, and toss well with spoons to fully coat.

The Verdict
This was our offering at a potluck dinner party, and they were well received. I liked the tartness from the lemon, combined with the velvety coating the butter and herbs provided. These are fun, different, and memorable—all good things to bring along to a potluck!

ITALIAN RICE

serves 4

The Ingredients

1 (14.5-ounce) can diced tomatoes, drained
6 green onions, sliced
2 garlic cloves, minced
1 teaspoon Italian seasoning
1 cup long-grain white basmati rice
2 cups chicken broth

The Directions

Use a 4-quart slow cooker. Put the tomatoes and sliced green onions into the bottom of your slow cooker. Add the garlic and Italian seasoning. Stir in the white rice until it's evenly coated with the tomatoes and spices. Pour on the chicken broth. Cover and cook on low for 4 hours, or until the rice is tender. Let the slow cooker sit with the lid off for 10 to 15 minutes before serving and fluff with a fork to release the steam.

The Verdict

This is a great side dish to serve with roasted chicken or a beef roast. The finished rice is speckled with red and green from the tomatoes and green onions. It appears fancy and complicated but is super easy to throw together.

PINEAPPLE SWEET POTATOES

serves 5

The Ingredients

4 to 6 medium sweet potatoes, peeled and cut in 2-inch chunks
2 tablespoons brown sugar
1 teaspoon ground nutmeg
1 teaspoon ground cinnamon
1 (20-ounce) can crushed pineapple (and juice)

The Directions

Use a 2-quart slow cooker. Toss the sweet potato cubes in your slow cooker with the brown sugar, nutmeg, and cinnamon. Pour the contents of the pineapple can on top. Cover and cook on low for 6 hours, high for 3 to 4, or until the sweet potatoes are tender.

The Verdict

Don't save sweet potatoes to eat only during the holidays! This is a delicious family-pleasing side dish to enjoy year-round. I was worried at first that the pineapple would be too sweet when combined with the sweet potatoes, but instead they provided a hint of tartness usually lacking in candied sweet potato dishes.

RED POTATOES WITH ROSEMARY AND GARLIC

serves 4

The Ingredients

1½ pounds baby red potatoes
4 garlic cloves, coarsely chopped
1½ teaspoons dried rosemary
2 tablespoons olive oil
½ teaspoon kosher salt
½ teaspoon black pepper

The Directions

Use a 4-quart slow cooker. Wash and quarter the red potatoes, and add to your slow cooker. I don't peel red potatoes, but you can if you'd like. Add the chopped garlic, rosemary, olive oil, salt, and pepper. Toss the potatoes with two large spoons to coat evenly with the oil and spices. Cover and cook on low for 4 hours, or on high for 2 hours. Your potatoes are done when they become fork-tender.

The Verdict

I love roasting potatoes in the slow cooker. They get caramelized the same way they do in the oven, but you don't need to check on them every few minutes to make sure they don't burn. This is a great side dish to prepare when grilling outdoors—there's no need to heat up the kitchen and no need to stay inside to monitor.

ROASTED GARLIC SPOONBREAD

serves 4 to 6

The Ingredients

3/4 cup yellow cornmeal
1 tablespoon sugar
1/2 teaspoon cayenne pepper
2 cups milk
2 tablespoons butter, melted
4 eggs
1/4 cup grated Parmesan cheese
1 head garlic, cloves peeled but intact (15 cloves)

The Directions

Use a 2-quart slow cooker. In a large mixing bowl, combine the cornmeal, sugar, cayenne, milk, melted butter, and eggs until a batter forms. Stir in the Parmesan cheese and whole garlic cloves. Pour the batter into the greased slow cooker. Cover and cook on low for 4 to 5 hours, or on high for 2 to 3. Your spoonbread is finished when the center is set and an inserted skewer comes out clean.

Serve warm alongside a roasted chicken breast or pork chop.

The Verdict

The garlic roasts inside the cornbread, creating a moist and savory side dish. The garlic was too pronounced for my children, so they ate around the cloves (you can see them easily). Adam and I absolutely loved the mild and smoky roasted garlic flavor and we ate our pieces without any butter, which we usually go overboard with when eating regular cornbread.

ROASTED ROOT VEGETABLES

serves 6

The Ingredients

1 medium sweet potato, peeled and cut in 1-inch chunks

2 large russet potatoes, peeled and cut in 1-inch chunks

2 large carrots, peeled and cut in 1-inch chunks (or a handful of baby carrots)

2 teaspoons dried rosemary

1/2 teaspoon kosher salt

1/2 teaspoon black pepper

2 tablespoons olive oil

The Directions

Use a 4-quart slow cooker. Plop the vegetables into the slow cooker and sprinkle the spices on top. Add the olive oil. Toss the vegetables well with spoons to coat them nicely with the olive oil and seasonings. Cover and cook on low for 6 hours, or on high for 3 to 4 hours. Your vegetables are done when they have reached the desired tenderness. I like mine to have a bit of a crunch.

The Verdict

This is an excellent side dish to serve alongside an oven-roasted chicken, barbecued tri-tip, or something similar. I like that I can roast vegetables in the slow cooker and not tie up my oven or heat up the house. I've found when making this during the summer months, my family ends up consuming more vegetables. We usually get most of our vegetable intake through tossed green salads during the summer, but after a few weeks in a row, the kids begin to revolt at eating salad *again*. This is a nice way to get them back on track.

"SCALLOPED" POTATOES

serves 4

The Ingredients
4 russet potatoes, peeled and sliced in half-inch rounds
kosher salt
pepper
onion powder
2 cups shredded cheddar cheese
2 (12-ounce) cans evaporated milk

The Directions
Use a 2-quart slow cooker. I know that I didn't list an amount for the salt, pepper, and onion powder. It's not a typo, I promise. Wash the potatoes well and slice. Put a layer of potato slices in the bottom of your slow cooker. Sprinkle on a bit of salt, pepper, and onion powder (I used three turns of the pepper grinder and a pinch of salt, and three shakes of the onion). Add a handful of cheese. Repeat the layers until you run out of potatoes and cheese. Pour the evaporated milk over the stack. Cover and cook on low for 8 hours, high for about 5, or until the potatoes are tender.

The Verdict
This beautiful and simple potato dish comes from Colleen, who was happy to pass along her Scottish grandmother's favorite recipe. Colleen writes that she only "recently discovered that scalloped potatoes do not contain cheese, or they would be considered au gratin potatoes, but her mother always called them 'scalloped,' and tradition is tradition." I agree.

SPAGHETTI SQUASH

serves 4

The Ingredients

1 (2- to 3-pound) spaghetti squash
4 tablespoons butter, melted
1/2 teaspoon ground thyme
1/2 teaspoon dried oregano
1/2 teaspoon kosher salt
1/4 teaspoon black pepper

The Directions

Use a 4-quart slow cooker. Cut the spaghetti squash in half. This is terribly difficult to do. If you microwave the squash on high for a minute or so, the skin will soften a bit, making cutting easier. Discard the seeds and place the squash halves into your slow cooker. It's okay to stack them. Combine the melted butter, thyme, oregano, salt, and pepper in a small bowl. Pour half of the butter mixture into each squash half. Cover and cook on low for 5 hours, or on high for 2 to 3. Your squash is done when you can fluff the flesh into stringy strands.

The Verdict

Spaghetti squash is a fun and healthy side dish, although I often use it as a main course for myself. My kids eat it with a bit of Parmesan sprinkled on top. I like that I can load it into the slow cooker in midafternoon and then leave to run errands or go to after-school sports practices. When in season, spaghetti squash is very inexpensive. If you want to continue eating it throughout the year, cut it in half, scoop out the seeds, and freeze the halves in a zippered plastic bag.

SUCCOTASH

serves 8

The Ingredients

1 (16-ounce) bag frozen corn
1 (16-ounce) bag frozen lima beans
1/4 cup chopped onion
2 vine-ripened tomatoes, diced
2 teaspoons sugar
1/4 teaspoon kosher salt
1/4 teaspoon black pepper
2 tablespoons butter

The Directions

Use a 4-quart slow cooker. Empty the bags of frozen vegetables into your slow cooker. Add the onion and tomatoes. Gingerly stir in (so the tomatoes don't turn to juice!) the sugar, salt, and pepper. Toss the pat of butter on top. Cover and cook on low for 6 hours, or on high for 2 to 3.

The Verdict

This reminded me of the vegetable mixture I was served in my elementary school cafeteria, but I'm happy to report it tasted MUCH better. We really should have eaten this while watching a Looney Tunes DVD, because it became quite apparent through our dinnertime conversation that my kids had no idea who Sylvester the Cat was. Ugh—I feel old.

VEGETARIAN MAIN COURSES

Baked Tofu   *68*

Bean and Cheese Burrito Casserole   *69*

Cheese Enchilada Stack   *70*

Eggplant Parmesan   *72*

Lemon Baked Tofu   *74*

Portobello Mushroom Sandwiches   *75*

Steak and Onions Tofu   *76*

Tofu "Fish" Cakes   *77*

Vegetable-Stuffed Peppers   *79*

Vegetarian Chili Shepherd's Pie   *80*

BAKED TOFU

serves 4

The Ingredients
    2 tablespoons olive oil
    1 (16-ounce) block extra-firm tofu
    3 tablespoons gluten-free soy sauce
    1 tablespoon sesame seeds

The Directions
Use a 2-quart slow cooker. Put the olive oil into the bottom of your slow cooker. Drain the tofu well, and slice into thin slices (I was able to get 10 slices). Put the tofu slices into your slow cooker, flipping each over a few times to coat both sides with oil. Add the soy sauce and sesame seeds, and flip the slices again to coat. Cover and cook on high for 2 to 3 hours. The tofu will be dry and "baked" when ready to serve.

The Verdict
I was surprised at how well this recipe worked in the slow cooker. My friend Danielle told me that this is how she prepares tofu, and I've made it quite a few times in the oven, but I have a tendency to overcook and burn it. Badly. The tofu baked nicely in the slow cooker, and became caramelized on the sides—the same way it does in the oven, but without needing to be babysat. I let it cool a bit, then the girls and I picked the pieces up and ate them with our fingers for an afternoon snack.

BEAN AND CHEESE BURRITO CASSEROLE

serves 8

The Ingredients

1 small onion, peeled and diced
1 green bell pepper, seeded and chopped
2 (14.5-ounce) cans diced tomatoes, undrained
1 (4-ounce) can roasted green chiles, undrained
1 teaspoon garlic powder
1/2 teaspoon chili powder
1/4 teaspoon ground cumin
8 flour or brown rice tortillas
4 cups cooked pinto beans (three 15-ounce cans, drained)
4 cups shredded Mexican blend cheese
sour cream, salsa, and avocado slices as garnish (optional)

The Directions

Use a 4-quart slow cooker. In a mixing bowl, stir together the onion, bell pepper, tomatoes, chiles, and spices. Put a layer of tortillas (you may need to tear them to get a nice fit) in the bottom of your slow cooker. Add a scoop of the onion and tomato mixture, and layer on a healthy spoonful of beans and a handful of cheese. Top with more tortillas. Repeat the layers two more times, finishing with a bunch of cheese on top. Cover and cook on low 6 to 7 hours. Cut into slices and serve with the desired toppings.

The Verdict

We all really liked this burrito casserole. I chose to keep it vegetarian, but if you've got some cooked chicken (page 299) or other meat in the fridge, go ahead and add in another layer! I opt to purchase shredded cheese when it's on sale and freeze the packages. If you shred your own cheese, your meal will be even lower in price.

CHEESE ENCHILADA STACK

serves 6

The Ingredients

1½ cups chicken broth *½ to ¾ c only*

1 (14.5-ounce) can crushed tomatoes

1 tablespoon chili powder

½ teaspoon dried oregano

½ teaspoon ground cumin

½ teaspoon garlic powder

½ teaspoon kosher salt

1 tablespoon dried minced onion or 1 small onion, finely diced

8 corn tortillas

4 cups shredded cheddar cheese

1 (4-ounce) can sliced olives, drained

6 tablespoons sour cream

The Directions

Use a 4-quart slow cooker. In a large mixing bowl, make the enchilada sauce by combining the broth, tomatoes, spices, and onion. Stir well and set aside. Put a layer of tortillas into the bottom of your slow cooker (you may need to tear a few). Add a handful of cheese and some sliced olives. Scoop a few large spoonfuls of enchilada sauce on top. Repeat the layers until you've run out of ingredients. Cover and cook on low for 5 to 6 hours, or until the cheese is melted, brown, and bubbly and the top layer has begun to pull away from the sides. Let sit unplugged with the cover off for 10 to 15 minutes. Serve with a dollop of sour cream.

The Verdict

We all cleaned our plates. It's a bit messy, but this is a great enchilada casserole. I chose to keep our meal vegetarian, but if you've got some cooked chicken, beef, or pork in the house, feel free to toss in an additional layer.

EGGPLANT PARMESAN

serves 4

The Ingredients

cooking spray

1 tablespoon olive oil

½ cup bread crumbs (I used Food for Life® bread)

2 teaspoons Italian seasoning

½ teaspoon kosher salt

¼ teaspoon black pepper

1 large eggplant, sliced (it's up to you if you'd like to peel it. I don't)

8 ounces mozzarella cheese, sliced

1 (26-ounce) jar prepared pasta sauce

The Directions

Use a 4-quart slow cooker sprayed with cooking spray. Pour the olive oil into a small bowl and set aside. Combine the bread crumbs, Italian seasoning, salt, and pepper in another bowl. Using a pastry brush, paint both sides of the sliced eggplant with olive oil, and sprinkle both sides with the bread crumb mixture. Put the eggplant slices into your slow cooker and top with mozzarella cheese. You will need to stagger stack the pieces to get them all inside. Pour the entire jar of pasta sauce over the top.

Cover and cook on low for 4 to 5 hours, or on high for 2 to 3 hours. Serve with a side of pasta and a green salad.

The Verdict

Eggplant Parmesan is one of my comfort foods. I could eat plateful after plateful of the stuff. Adam and the kids aren't quite as enthusiastic, but they do eat it to make me happy. I appreciate how nicely the eggplant cooks in the slow cooker, and how it doesn't get soggy. If you'd prefer a bit of a crunchy texture, you can pan-fry the bread crumb–coated slices before putting them into the slow cooker, but I usually omit this step to save time. You can save even more money by using home-made marinara sauce (page 298) instead of using store-bought sauce.

LEMON BAKED TOFU

serves 4

The Ingredients

1 (16-ounce) block extra-firm tofu
1/4 cup cornstarch
1 to 2 tablespoons butter
1 tablespoon gluten-free soy sauce
1 1/2 tablespoons sugar
2 tablespoons lemon juice
1 teaspoon dry mustard
1 teaspoon dried basil
1 teaspoon ground thyme

The Directions

Use a 2-quart slow cooker. Drain the tofu well and chop into bite-size chunks. Shake with the cornstarch in a ziplock freezer bag until coated. Pan-fry on the stove in butter until the tofu is a golden color and the outside begins to crisp. Set aside.

In a mixing bowl, combine the soy sauce, sugar, lemon juice, mustard, basil, and thyme. Put the tofu into the slow cooker and pour the sauce over the top. Toss the tofu a few times with spoons to coat evenly. Cover and cook on high for 2 to 3 hours, or until heated through and the flavors have melded. Serve with brown rice or quinoa.

The Verdict

Lemony and delicious. This sauce has a lot of flavor and nicely coats the tofu. This is a fantastic light meal. If you're not a fan of tofu, try this sauce with chicken thighs or pork chops.

PORTOBELLO MUSHROOM SANDWICHES

serves 4

The Ingredients

4 large portobello mushrooms, stems removed

1/4 cup prepared Italian salad dressing

1 (7-ounce) jar roasted red peppers

buns, rolls, or toasted bread for serving

The Directions

Use a 4-quart slow cooker. Wash the mushrooms, and remove and discard the stems. Place the mushrooms in the bottom of your slow cooker. Add the salad dressing and the entire jar of roasted peppers. Cover and cook on low for 4 to 5 hours, or on high for about 2 hours. Serve with a slotted spoon onto buns, rolls, or toasted bread.

The Verdict

The tangy flavor from the salad dressing and the peppers complemented the thick "meaty" texture of the mushrooms beautifully. I really liked these sandwiches a lot, and so did Adam. The kids thought they were kind of weird, but ate enough to make me happy.

STEAK AND ONIONS TOFU

serves 2

The Ingredients

1 large onion, sliced in rings
1 (16-ounce) package extra-firm tofu
¼ cup cornstarch
2 to 3 tablespoons butter
2 tablespoons balsamic vinegar
1 tablespoon A-1® steak sauce
1 tablespoon water

The Directions

Use a 2-quart slow cooker. Put the onion rings into the bottom of an empty slow cooker.

Drain the tofu well and chop into bite-size chunks. Shake with the cornstarch in a ziplock freezer bag until coated. Pan-fry on the stove in butter until the tofu is a golden color and the outside begins to crisp.

Put the tofu into the slow cooker, and add the vinegar, steak sauce, and water. Toss the tofu and onion with spoons to cover them completely with the sauce.

Cover and cook on high for 2 to 3 hours, or until the onion has reached the desired tenderness.

The Verdict

Who would have thought tofu could taste like a steak? If you're a new vegetarian or are trying to cut back on your meat consumption, this is a great gateway dish.

TOFU "FISH" CAKES

serves 4

The Ingredients

1 (16-ounce) package extra-firm tofu
¼ cup cornstarch
2 to 3 tablespoons butter
4 garlic cloves, minced
2 teaspoons Old Bay seasoning (or make your own, recipe follows)
2 lemons, cut in wedges, for serving
tartar sauce for serving

The Directions

Use a 2-quart slow cooker. Drain the tofu well, and chop into bite-size chunks. Shake with the cornstarch in a ziplock freezer bag until coated. Pan-fry on the stove in butter until the tofu is a golden color and the outside begins to crisp.

Place the tofu into a slow cooker, and add the minced garlic and Old Bay. Cover and cook on high for 2 to 3 hours. Squeeze on the lemon at the table and serve with tartar sauce.

The Verdict

The kids and I ate this for an afternoon snack and really enjoyed ourselves. The texture of the tofu mimics fish or crab cakes, which is neat.

If you don't have Old Bay seasoning on hand, you can make your own blend to store in the cupboard.

(CONTINUED)

OLD BAY–TYPE SEASONING

makes ¼ cup

1 tablespoon ground bay leaves
2 teaspoons celery salt
1½ teaspoons dry mustard
1 teaspoon black pepper
1 teaspoon paprika
½ teaspoon ground celery seed
½ teaspoon white pepper
½ teaspoon ground nutmeg
½ teaspoon ground ginger
¼ teaspoon ground allspice
¼ teaspoon ground cloves
¼ teaspoon crushed red pepper flakes

Combine spices and store in an air-tight container in a cool dry place.

VEGETABLE-STUFFED PEPPERS

serves 6

The Ingredients

6 bell peppers (your choice of colors!)
$1/2$ cup prepared pasta sauce
1 (15-ounce) can black beans, drained and rinsed
1 (8-ounce) can corn, drained
1 small onion, diced
2 cups cooked long-grain rice
$1/2$ teaspoon smoked paprika
$1/4$ teaspoon kosher salt
$1/4$ teaspoon black pepper
1 cup shredded cheese (I used a cheddar mixture)
$1/3$ cup water

The Directions

Use a 6-quart slow cooker. Cut the tops off the peppers, and remove the seeds and cores. In a mixing bowl, combine the pasta sauce, beans, corn, onion, rice, spices, and cheese. The mixture will be quite gloppy. Spoon as much of this filling as you can into each pepper. Snuggle the peppers down into the slow cooker. Carefully pour the water around the base of the peppers. Cover and cook on low for 6 to 8 hours, or on high for 3 to 4.

The Verdict

These peppers taste great. The filling worked really well, and the peppers softened and steamed well in the crock without falling apart. I shared the peppers with my mom and grandma, who also really liked them. Adam ate one, but also had some leftover pot roast, and the girls each tried a bite, but mostly ate quesadillas while watching *Project Runway* with me.

VEGETARIAN CHILI SHEPHERD'S PIE

serves 6

The Ingredients

1 (15-ounce) can black beans, drained and rinsed

1 (15-ounce) can kidney beans, drained and rinsed

1 (16-ounce) package frozen corn

1 small onion, diced

1 (15-ounce) can tomato sauce

1 teaspoon ground cumin

1/2 teaspoon kosher salt

1/2 teaspoon black pepper

1 cup shredded cheddar cheese

2 cups leftover mashed potatoes

1/2 teaspoon smoked paprika

The Directions

Use a 4-quart slow cooker. Drain and rinse the beans, and add to the slow cooker. Add the corn and diced onion. Pour in the tomato sauce, add the cumin, salt, and pepper, and stir to combine. Sprinkle on the shredded cheese. Add the mashed potatoes to the top of the cheese, flattening with the back of a spoon or your hand. Dust with smoked paprika.

Cover and cook on low for 6 hours, or on high for 3 to 4 hours. Uncover the slow cooker and cook on high for 20 to 30 minutes to cook away any accumulated condensation.

The Verdict

This is a great way to use up leftover mashed potatoes and to clean out your pantry. Feel free to switch the beans to your family favorites, or use drained canned corn instead of the frozen. The little bit of smoked paprika provides quite a smoky punch. If you're purchasing it for the first time, you can also use it in Poor Man's Chili (page 52) and the vegan Sweet Potato Chili (page 231).

POULTRY

Easy Peanut Butter Chicken   *82*

General Tso's Chicken   *83*

Honey Garlic Chicken   *84*

Marmalade Curry Chicken   *85*

Moroccan Chicken with Lentils   *86*

EASY PEANUT BUTTER CHICKEN

serves 4

The Ingredients

1½ pounds boneless, skinless chicken, cut in chunks (I like thighs)
½ cup natural peanut butter (creamy or chunky, your choice)
1 red bell pepper, seeded and sliced
1 large onion, coarsely chopped
1 tablespoon ground cumin
1 lime, juiced
¼ cup gluten-free soy sauce
½ cup chicken broth

The Directions

Use a 4-quart slow cooker. Put the chicken in the bottom of your cooker. Add the peanut butter. Toss in the vegetables and cumin. Squeeze in lime, and add soy sauce and chicken broth. Stir to combine. Cover and cook on low for 6 to 8 hours, or on high for 4 hours. Serve over brown or white basmati rice.

The Verdict

Adam and I thought this tasted like the chicken served at our favorite Thai restaurant. We absolutely loved it, and so did our girls. You can add red pepper flakes at the table if you'd like some heat. The bite of citrus that comes from the lime is divine. Yum!

GENERAL TSO'S CHICKEN

serves 4

The Ingredients

1 pound boneless, skinless chicken, cut in 1-inch chunks
4 garlic cloves, minced
3 tablespoons brown sugar
1 teaspoon dried ginger
2 tablespoons gluten-free soy sauce
1/2 teaspoon crushed red pepper flakes
1 (16-ounce) package stir-fry vegetables (to add later)

The Directions

Use a 4-quart slow cooker. Put the chicken into the bottom of your slow cooker and add the garlic, brown sugar, ginger, soy sauce, and red pepper flakes. Toss the chicken with two spoons to coat it evenly. Cover and cook on low for 5 to 6 hours, then add the frozen stir-fry vegetables. Re-cover and cook on high for 1 hour, or until the vegetables are heated through. Serve over white or brown basmati rice.

The Verdict

My kids really liked this chicken, and ate most of it themselves. General Tso's chicken served in restaurants is usually breaded and deep-fried, which is not healthy and laden with gluten. This take-out fake-out version is much better for your heart, and your wallet.

HONEY GARLIC CHICKEN

serves 4

The Ingredients

1½ pounds boneless, skinless chicken thighs
3 garlic cloves, chopped
1 teaspoon dried basil
½ cup gluten-free soy sauce
½ cup ketchup
⅓ cup honey

The Directions

Use a 4-quart slow cooker. Put the chicken into your cooker. In a small bowl, combine the rest of the ingredients, then pour evenly on top of the chicken. Cover and cook on low for 6 to 8 hours, or on high for 3 to 4 hours. Serve over basmati rice with your favorite steamed vegetables.

The Verdict

This is the new favorite chicken recipe in our household. The salty sweet taste is a hit with the kids, and they ask for additional helpings, which is a surefire way to make Mom happy and get out of doing the dishes. If you buy chicken in bulk, this is an easy TV dinner meal to make ahead of time in a plastic zippered freezer bag as described on page 6.

MARMALADE CURRY CHICKEN

serves 4

The Ingredients

4 boneless, skinless chicken breast halves
1 (18-ounce) jar orange marmalade
1½ teaspoons curry powder
½ teaspoon cayenne pepper
¼ teaspoon ground ginger
¼ teaspoon kosher salt
¼ cup chicken broth

The Directions

Use a 4-quart slow cooker. Put the chicken breasts into the bottom of your slow cooker. In a mixing bowl, combine the orange marmalade, spices, and chicken broth. Pour this sauce evenly over the top of the chicken breasts. Cover and cook on low for 6 to 7 hours, or on high for 4 hours. Serve over brown basmati rice.

The Verdict

This fantastic chicken recipe comes from Danielle, an EMT in New Jersey. Due to her sporadic schedule, she appreciates being able to throw together a healthy meal within minutes, and leave the house knowing she'll return to a great dinner. Chicken breasts can become terribly dry when cooked in the oven or on the stovetop, but when slow cooked they are tender and juicy.

MOROCCAN CHICKEN WITH LENTILS

serves 6

The Ingredients

1½ cups lentils
2 garlic cloves, minced
½ teaspoon kosher salt
¾ teaspoon turmeric
½ teaspoon cayenne pepper
½ teaspoon ground cinnamon
1 (8-ounce) package baby carrots
1½ pounds chicken (I used quarters with bones)
1 quart chicken broth

The Directions

Use a 6-quart slow cooker. Rinse the lentils and put them into the bottom of your slow cooker. Add the garlic and spices. Use a spoon to mix the spices around in the lentils. Add the baby carrots and lay the chicken pieces on top. Pour in the broth. Cover and cook on low for 7 to 8 hours, or until the lentils have reached the desired tenderness and the chicken is fully cooked.

The Verdict

Adam and I ate this meal by ourselves on a night the girls were at Grandma's, and then packed the leftovers up for the freezer. Lentils are filling, cheap, and when prepared like this, tasty. I used to be scared to incorporate lentils into my meal plan because I thought they tasted a bit like dirt. You can remove much of this "earthy" flavor by rinsing them thoroughly in running water before cooking.

BEEF & PORK

Carnitas *88*

Juicy Beefy Burgers *89*

Layered Ground Beef Casserole *90*

Maple-Glazed Pork Chops *91*

Pioneer Dinner *92*

Sticky Chops *93*

CARNITAS

serves 6

The Ingredients

½ tablespoon kosher salt

1 tablespoon ground cumin

2 pounds pork shoulder

7 whole garlic cloves

½ cup freshly squeezed orange juice (about 1 large orange)

¼ cup freshly squeezed lime juice (about 1 large lime)

½ cup beef broth

corn tortillas

sour cream, salsa, and sliced avocado (optional)

The Directions

Use a 6-quart slow cooker. In a small bowl, combine the salt and cumin. Rub the mixture all over the pork, then plop into the slow cooker. Add the whole garlic cloves. Squeeze on the citrus juices, and pour the beef broth evenly over the top.

Cook on low for 8 to 10 hours, or until the pork shreds quite easily with a fork. If your meat is still fully intact after 8 hours, remove and cut into chunks, then return to the crock and flip to high for about an hour or two.

Shred the meat fully and serve on warmed corn tortillas with the desired toppings.

The Verdict

This is so totally good. I adored the citrusy flavor of the meat and the slight smokiness from the cumin. If you don't eat pork, you can use a beef chuck roast instead of the pork shoulder. I was happy to discover through this recipe that I'm no longer allergic to pork. This past pregnancy must have tweaked my body chemistry—something I'm thrilled about!

JUICY BEEFY BURGERS

serves 4

The Ingredients

1 pound lean ground meat
$\frac{1}{2}$ teaspoon garlic powder
$\frac{1}{2}$ teaspoon seasoned salt
$\frac{1}{2}$ teaspoon black pepper
$\frac{1}{4}$ cup beef broth

The Directions

Use a 6-quart slow cooker. In a mixing bowl, mix together the ground meat with the garlic powder, salt, and pepper. Form into 4 patties, and place on the bottom of your slow cooker insert. Pour the beef broth over the top. Cover and cook on low for 5 hours, or until the meat is cooked through. Serve on buns like a hamburger, or directly on your plate like Salisbury steak.

The Verdict

This is a fantastic way to make moist and juicy burgers with very little effort. I used ground venison our neighbors gave us, and the meat turned out nice and juicy. We ate our "Salisbury steak" with a fork and knife, and dipped the meat into a puddle of mustard. I often serve hamburgers open-faced on a lightly salted rice cake. The crunch is wonderful.

LAYERED GROUND BEEF CASSEROLE

serves 6 to 8

The Ingredients

3 large russet potatoes, peeled and thinly sliced
1 onion, diced
1 cup frozen corn
1 green bell pepper, seeded and chopped
1 pound lean ground beef, browned and drained
$\frac{1}{2}$ teaspoon seasoned salt
1 (8-ounce) can tomato sauce
1 cup shredded cheddar cheese

The Directions

Use a 6-quart slow cooker. Place the potatoes on the bottom of your slow cooker insert. Add the onion, frozen corn, and bell pepper. Evenly distribute the browned ground beef over the vegetables. Sprinkle on the seasoned salt. Pour the tomato sauce over the top, and add the cheddar cheese. Cover and cook on low for 8 hours, or on high for about 4 hours.

The Verdict

This is a tasty, inexpensive, layered casserole to have in your monthly meal plan. If you have leftovers, they are great reheated the next day or frozen for an additional meal. Feel free to switch around the vegetables to whatever you have on hand in the freezer, or to cater to your family favorites.

MAPLE-GLAZED PORK CHOPS

serves 4

The Ingredients

4 pork chops
1/3 cup maple syrup
1/3 cup chicken broth
2 teaspoons apple cider vinegar
1 teaspoon dry mustard

The Directions

Use a 4-quart slow cooker. Put the chops into the slow cooker. Pour the maple syrup, chicken broth, and vinegar over the top of them. Add the mustard. Cover and cook on low for 6 to 8 hours, or until the chops are thoroughly cooked and have reached the desired tenderness.

The Verdict

These chops are very maple flavored, which is great if you like maple syrup. I try to stick to natural maple syrup, even though it is much more expensive than the imitation stuff. I buy it in large bottles at Costco or Trader Joe's, use it mostly for cooking or baking, and have the kids dip their pancakes and waffles into honey, which is much cheaper.

PIONEER DINNER

serves 6

The Ingredients

4 large carrots, peeled and chopped into 2-inch chunks
1 yellow onion, peeled and coarsely chopped
4 brown baking potatoes, chopped into 2-inch chunks (I didn't peel them)
4 Italian-flavored sausages, sliced in 1-inch pieces
1 cup beef broth

The Directions

Use a 6-quart slow cooker. Layer the ingredients into the slow cooker in this order: carrots, onion, potatoes, and sausage. Pour the broth evenly over the top. Cover and cook on low for 6 to 8 hours, or until the vegetables have reached the desired tenderness.

The Verdict

This is a filling, inexpensive meal that is super easy to pull together on a busy morning. The seasoning from the sausage is enough to flavor the vegetables without any additional spices. I make this dinner about once a month, and try to keep the ingredients on hand. My girls like eating "like Laura and Mary do" in the *Little House on the Prairie* books.

STICKY CHOPS

serves 4

The Ingredients

4 pork chops
4 garlic cloves, minced
1/3 cup apple juice
2 tablespoons honey
1 tablespoon gluten-free soy sauce

The Directions

Use a 4-quart slow cooker. Put the chops into the slow cooker. Top with the minced garlic, apple juice, honey, and soy sauce. No need to stir—everything will meld on its own. Cover and cook on low for 6 to 8 hours, or until the chops are thoroughly cooked and have reached the desired tenderness.

The Verdict

If you're craving chops with an Asian flair, this is the recipe for you. The meat is nicely infused with flavor. This is a great candidate for slow cooker TV dinners (page 6).

DESSERTS

Baked Maple Apple Halves   95

Caramel Fondue   96

Cinnamon Raisin Rice Pudding   97

Lemon Pudding Cake   98

Mint Chocolate Fondue   99

Peanut Butter Cup Cake   100

Scalloped Apples   102

Sticky Cereal Dessert   103

Vanilla Custard   104

BAKED MAPLE APPLE HALVES

serves 4

The Ingredients

2 large apples, cored and cut in half (I used Fuji)
2 tablespoons butter
$\frac{1}{2}$ cup orange juice
2 tablespoons maple syrup
4 tablespoons sweetened whipped cream (from a can!)

The Directions

Use a 6-quart slow cooker. Put the apple halves into the bottom of your slow cooker, flesh-side up. In a small bowl, melt the butter in the microwave. Stir in the orange juice and maple syrup. Spoon the butter and syrup mixture evenly into the apple halves. Cover and cook on low for 2 to 3 hours, or on high for 1 to 2 hours. I cooked our apples on high for 1 hour and 20 minutes. Serve with a dollop of sweetened whipped cream.

The Verdict

This is a great easy dessert to make during the week. It's really hard (for me) to make desserts during the week—it's all I can do to get dinner on the table! But we've usually got the ingredients for these apples in the house, and I like that they aren't laden with sugar. It's a nice surprise for the kids after bath time.

CARAMEL FONDUE

serves 12

The Ingredients

1 (14-ounce) can sweetened condensed milk
1 cup light corn syrup
2 cups packed brown sugar
2 tablespoons water
1 teaspoon vanilla extract
6 Granny Smith apples, sliced

The Directions

Use a 2-quart slow cooker. Pour the sweetened condensed milk (don't forget to lick the can!) and corn syrup into your slow cooker. Add the brown sugar, water, and vanilla. Cover and cook on low for 4 hours, or on high for 1 to 2 hours. Stir well and serve with tart apple slices.

The Verdict

This is addictingly good. It's super sweet, but not sweet enough that you can't justify eating the entire crockful. I made this dip for a group of third graders, who were absolutely thrilled with their afternoon snack. Brush your teeth really well after eating!

CINNAMON RAISIN RICE PUDDING

serves 4

The Ingredients

3 cups milk
1/3 cup Arborio rice
1/4 cup sugar
1 teaspoon vanilla extract
1/2 cup raisins

The Directions

Use a 2-quart slow cooker. Put the milk into the slow cooker and add the rice. Stir in the sugar, vanilla, and raisins. Cover and cook on low for 5 to 6 hours, on high for 2 to 3, or until the rice is tender and thickened like pudding.

The Verdict

The finished pudding is marvelous—rich and creamy, and the raisins get all plump and juicy. Delicious! Arborio rice Is very short-grained and is usually used for making risotto (see page 238). You can find it in a box in the rice aisle of your grocery store.

LEMON PUDDING CAKE

serves 6

The Ingredients

cooking spray
1 cup sugar
¼ cup all-purpose flour (I used Pamela's Baking Mix)
¼ teaspoon kosher salt
1 cup 2 percent buttermilk
¼ cup fresh lemon juice
3 eggs, whisked
1 teaspoon vanilla extract

The Directions

Use a 4-quart slow cooker coated with cooking spray. In a mixing bowl, whisk together the sugar, flour, and salt. Set aside. In a separate bowl, whisk together the wet ingredients. Pour the buttermilk mixture slowly into the dry ingredients and continue mixing to form a batter. Scrape the cake batter into your slow cooker. Cover and cook on high for 2 to 4 hours, or until the cake has set in the center, browned, and pulled away from the sides. Test with a toothpick to ensure doneness, and let the cake sit, unplugged and uncovered, for 20 minutes before serving.

The Verdict

Oh-my-lemon-goodness! The cake separates from the lemon pudding and floats to the top and puffs up. The pudding underneath is quite lemony and thickens nicely.

MINT CHOCOLATE FONDUE

serves 8

The Ingredients

12 ounces semisweet chocolate chips
1/2 cup heavy cream
1/2 teaspoon mint extract or 2 tablespoons peppermint schnapps
marshmallows or cookies for serving

The Directions

Use a 2-quart slow cooker. Put the chocolate chips into your slow cooker. Add the heavy cream and mint extract (or the schnapps). Cover and cook on low for 2 hours, stirring every 30 minutes. Serve with marshmallows or cookies for dipping.

The Verdict

This tastes exactly like liquid Girl Scout cookies. It's perfectly minty—not too much, not too little. We used marshmallows for our fondue dippers.

PEANUT BUTTER CUP CAKE

serves 8

The Ingredients

cooking spray
1 cup all-purpose flour (I used Pamela's Baking Mix)
1 cup sugar (divided)
1 teaspoon baking powder
$\frac{1}{2}$ teaspoon kosher salt
$\frac{1}{2}$ cup creamy peanut butter
$\frac{1}{2}$ cup milk
1 tablespoon canola oil
1 teaspoon vanilla extract
3 tablespoons unsweetened cocoa powder
1 cup boiling water

The Directions

Use a 4-quart slow cooker coated with cooking spray. In a mixing bowl, combine the flour, $\frac{1}{2}$ cup sugar, the baking powder, and salt. Melt the peanut butter for 30 seconds in the microwave, and add to the mix with the milk, oil, and vanilla. Stir well to combine. Spread the peanut butter cake batter into your slow cooker.

In a separate bowl, combine the cocoa powder, the remaining $\frac{1}{2}$ cup of sugar, and the boiling water. Mix well and pour evenly over the batter in your cooker.

Cover and cook on high for 2 to 4 hours, or until the top has set and an inserted toothpick comes out clean. Let the cake sit uncovered in the unplugged cooker for about 20 minutes, then serve warm in dessert bowls.

The Verdict

If you like peanut butter with your chocolate, or chocolate with your peanut butter (one of the best ad campaigns ever . . .) you will absolutely love this cake. The peanut butter–flavored cake floats to the top, leaving a layer of molten chocolate gooeyness underneath.

SCALLOPED APPLES

serves 8

The Ingredients

    4 Granny Smith apples
    4 Golden Delicious apples
    1 cup sugar
    1/2 teaspoon ground cinnamon
    1/2 teaspoon ground cloves
    1/4 cup butter, sliced
    vanilla ice cream (for serving)

The Directions

Use a 4-quart slow cooker. Peel, core, and slice the apples. Place into a slow cooker, and toss with the sugar, cinnamon, cloves, and butter slices. Cover and cook on low for 4 to 5 hours. Serve hot with a scoop of vanilla ice cream.

The Verdict

This is pretty much apple pie filling without the crust. Lovely. The tartness from the Granny Smith apples balances out the sweetness of the Golden Delicious, which creates a winning combination. If you'd like, you can cook for a few more hours to make applesauce.

STICKY CEREAL DESSERT

serves 10

The Ingredients

cooking spray
8 cups Rice Chex cereal
1 cup salted peanuts
1 (14-ounce) can sweetened condensed milk
1 teaspoon vanilla extract

The Directions

Use a 6-quart slow cooker. Spray your stoneware insert with cooking spray. Pour all the ingredients into your slow cooker and stir well to combine. Cover and cook on high for 2 hours, stirring every 20 minutes. When the cooking time has elapsed, spread the contents onto a length of wax paper. Let cool completely, then break into chunks. The finished product will be gooey and sticky. Store in the refrigerator.

The Verdict

This was an experiment that didn't go exactly as I planned. I was hoping the condensed milk would harden more when cooked and create a super simple brittle. Instead, I got a Chex cereal bar without the bar. The kids adored this and begged me to make it again a week later. My grandma is also a big fan, which means that my mistake ended up actually working. Go figure.

VANILLA CUSTARD

serves 6 to 8

The Ingredients

4 eggs
½ cup sugar (I like baker's sugar because the granules are fine)
1 tablespoon vanilla extract
⅛ teaspoon kosher salt
3 cups nonfat milk
1 teaspoon ground nutmeg

The Directions

Use a 6-quart slow cooker with an inserted 1½ -quart casserole dish (Pyrex®, Corningware®). Add water around the dish until halfway up the side. You are using the slow cooker as a bain-marie, or water bath.

In a large mixing bowl, whisk together the eggs, sugar, vanilla, and salt. In a glass measuring cup, heat the milk for 2 minutes on high in the microwave. Slowly whisk the heated milk into the egg and sugar mixture. Go slowly, or you'll scramble the eggs! Pour everything into the inserted casserole dish. Sprinkle nutmeg over the top.

Cover and cook on high for 2 to 4 hours. The custard should be set but still a bit jiggly. Touch lightly with your finger to test. When set, unplug the slow cooker and let it sit with the lid off until the casserole dish has cooled enough to remove safely. Chill in the refrigerator for 2 to 3 hours before serving.

The Verdict

This is a recipe from Joyce in Portland, Oregon. Her daughter Norah writes that she remembers her mom making it all the time while she was growing up, and she loves how easy it is to prepare in the slow cooker. We all adored this and ate it in one sitting. I love that such a scrumptious dessert was made using fat-free milk. Thank you, Joyce and Norah!

$10
and
Under

The difference between \$7 and \$10 seems minimal—it's only \$3, but I found a huge difference when shopping for the recipes featured here, compared to the first section. The quality of the meat and produce remained the same—but both the quantity and variety rose significantly.

In this \$10 and under section, you will find that you can throw together very filling main courses, fun desserts, and side dishes for entertaining. You'll also find that your protein choices have expanded to incorporate fish, turkey, and pork shoulder. As is true throughout the book, most of these meals provide enough food for leftovers, always a bonus for me!

As stressed in the Introduction, the prices here reflect using store-bought broth, canned tomatoes, and dried herbs. You can significantly reduce your shopping receipts by making your own broth from scratch or by using bouillon, and by using tomatoes and herbs from your garden. The rule of thumb is to double the measurement of fresh herbs compared to dried.

BEVERAGES

Coconut Hot Chocolate   *109*

Witch's Brew   *110*

COCONUT HOT CHOCOLATE

serves 8

The Ingredients

    4 cups low-fat milk
    1 (14-ounce) can unsweetened coconut milk
    1 (14-ounce) can sweetened condensed milk
    3 tablespoons unsweetened cocoa powder
    1 teaspoon vanilla extract
    whipped cream as garnish (optional)

The Directions

Use a 4-quart slow cooker. Combine all the milks and the cocoa powder. Stir in the vanilla extract. Cover and cook on low for 4 to 5 hours, or on high for 1 to 2. Serve hot with a dollop of whipped cream, if desired. If serving guests, leave the crock lid off with the pot on low. Your drink will not stay hot enough on warm with the lid off.

The Verdict

Drinking this is like taking a mini vacation without the expense or jet lag.

WITCH'S BREW

serves 8 to 10

The Ingredients

2 quarts apple juice

2 quarts pineapple juice (or thereabouts: a can holds 1 quart, 14 ounces)

¼ teaspoon allspice

1 (6-ounce) box lime Jell-O

5 to 6 whole star anise (see Note)

orange sherbet for serving

Note: I wouldn't go out of my way to purchase star anise if you don't already have it in the house. It looks neat floating in the pot (like little spiders) and provides a touch of licorice taste, but not enough to justify the expense. If you really want a tad of licorice flavor, throw in a few licorice jelly beans and call it a day.

The Directions

Use a 6-quart slow cooker. Pour in the juices and add the allspice. Stir in the Jell-O powder and float the star anise, if using, on top. Cover and cook on low for about 5 hours, or on high for about 3 hours. Serve with a scoop of orange sherbet—it will cool the beverage down enough for small children to enjoy right away, and creates a fun foamy/slimy film on top.

The Verdict

We had a playdate a few days before Halloween, and my five-year-old taste testers couldn't get enough of this stuff. The comments I overheard were priceless:

"It doesn't taste like there are spiders or lizards or bugs in it."

"How did your mom even know how to make this?"

"Is my tongue green yet?"

"I've never had ice cream in a drink before."
"I guess this is why witches have green faces."

This is a super easy hot beverage to whip up, and tastes like a lovely citrus cocktail. My little friends were thrilled with their after-school snack (I promise I fed them lunch before filling them with sugar!), and I received many sticky hugs and thank-yous.

BREAKFASTS

Apple-Pecan Bread Pudding *113*

Raisin Nut Oatmeal *115*

Southwestern Hash Brown Bake *116*

Ultimate Breakfast Casserole *117*

APPLE-PECAN BREAD PUDDING

serves 6

The Ingredients

cooking spray

4 cups toasted bread cubes (approximately 8 slices; I used gluten-free bread)

2 Granny Smith apples, peeled, cored, and diced

1/4 cup butter, melted

1/2 cup coarsely chopped pecans

1 cup raisins

1 cup brown sugar

2 teaspoons pumpkin pie spice

3 eggs

2 cups half-and-half

The Directions

Use a 2-quart slow cooker. Spray your stoneware insert well with cooking spray. Put the toasted bread cubes into your cooker and add the diced apples. Toss the bread and apples with the melted butter. Dump in the pecans, raisins, and brown sugar, and sprinkle in the pumpkin pie spice. Stir gingerly to distribute the ingredients evenly. In a mixing bowl, whisk together the eggs and half-and-half, and pour evenly over the top of the assembled ingredients. Cover and cook on low for 4 to 5 hours, or on high for 3 to 4 hours. Your pudding is done when it has browned on top and pulled away from the sides. The center should be set and not super jiggly. Serve warm with vanilla ice cream as a dessert or plain for breakfast.

(CONTINUED)

The Verdict

In a perfect world, little fairies would assemble this in the middle of the night so I could eat it every morning. I'd like them to set up the coffeepot, too. This makes six hearty grown-up–sized portions. This is plenty of food for one full week of kid breakfasts. Store in a covered container in the refrigerator, and reheat in the microwave with a touch of milk.

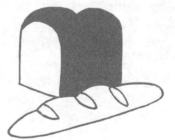

RAISIN NUT OATMEAL

serves 4

The Ingredients

    2 cups certified gluten-free rolled oats
    4 cups milk
    ½ cup raisins
    ¼ cup chopped walnuts or almonds
    1 teaspoon ground cinnamon
    2 tablespoons brown sugar

The Directions

Use a 2-quart slow cooker. Combine the oats and milk in your slow cooker, and stir in the raisins, nuts, cinnamon, and sugar. Cover and cook on low for 2 to 3 hours, on high for 1 to 2 hours, or until the desired consistency is reached. I like my oats to still have some chewiness to them.

The Verdict

Every time I eat oatmeal, I think I really should eat it more often. This is filling and hearty, and won't leave you hungry an hour later. Oatmeal comes out nice and creamy in the slow cooker—I love it prepared this way.

SOUTHWESTERN HASH BROWN BAKE

serves 8

The Ingredients

1 (30-ounce) bag frozen hash brown potatoes

6 eggs

4 large turkey sausages, diced (mild or spicy, your choice)

1 (12-ounce) can evaporated milk

1 (10-ounce) can tomatoes and chiles (Rotel)

1/2 teaspoon kosher salt

1/4 teaspoon black pepper

2 cups Mexican blend shredded cheese

salsa, sour cream, or sliced avocado for serving (optional)

The Directions

Use a 6-quart slow cooker. Put the frozen hash browns into your slow cooker. In a large mixing bowl, whisk together the eggs, sausages, milk, tomatoes, salt, pepper, and cheese. Pour this mixture evenly on top of the potatoes. Cover your cooker and cook on low for 7 hours, or on high for 3 to 4 hours. Serve with salsa, sour cream, or sliced avocado, if you'd like.

The Verdict

This is a wonderful recipe to serve to out-of-town guests. I like to assemble everything the night before and plug in the slow cooker right before going to bed. I also load up the coffeepot, so if my guests wake up bright and early, they can serve themselves without fuss. I've left this casserole on warm successfully for an additional 4 hours.

ULTIMATE BREAKFAST CASSEROLE

serves 10 to 12

The Ingredients

12 slices bacon, cooked and crumbled
4 cups toasted (or stale) bread cubes (I used bread made from a gluten-free bread mix)
cooking spray
2 cups shredded cheese (I used a 4-cheese Mexican blend)
8 ounces sliced mushrooms
8 eggs
1½ cups milk (I used fat-free cow's, but any would work just fine)
½ teaspoon kosher salt
½ teaspoon black pepper

The Directions

Use a 6-quart slow cooker. Cook the bacon to the desired crispiness and toast the bread. Set these aside. Spray the inside of your slow cooker with cooking spray and set that aside, too.

In a large mixing bowl, combine the shredded cheese, mushrooms, eggs, milk, salt, and pepper.

Put the bread cubes into the bottom of your sprayed slow cooker, and pour the egg mixture evenly over the entire thing. Place the bacon pieces on top.

Cover and cook on low for 6 to 8 hours, or until the eggs have set, or on high for about 3 to 4 hours. When the eggs have completely set, and your casserole has begun to brown on top and pull away from the sides, take the lid off the cooker and let the steam and moisture evaporate for about 15 minutes before serving.

(CONTINUED)

The Verdict

This is a wonderful breakfast casserole—it has pretty much everything you can imagine in it, and I was very close to calling it "kitchen sink breakfast casserole," but the girls thought that was kind of weird. So, it's THE ULTIMATE. Everyone in our house loved this casserole, and my grandma ate the leftovers and reported that they were fantastic.

This would be a welcome addition to a brunch or to serve to overnight guests.

APPETIZERS

Big Barbecue Little Smokies   *120*

Double Artichoke Dip   *121*

Fruit and Horseradish Cream Cheese Spread   *122*

Orange-Glazed Meatballs   *123*

Wasabi Almonds   *124*

BIG BARBECUE LITTLE SMOKIES

serves 8

The Ingredients

1 pound Little Smokies sausage
$^{1}/_{2}$ cup ketchup
$^{1}/_{2}$ cup brown sugar
1 teaspoon gluten-free Worcestershire sauce
$^{1}/_{2}$ cup barbecue sauce

The Directions

Use a 4-quart slow cooker. Put the sausage into your stoneware insert, and add the ketchup, brown sugar, Worcestershire sauce, and barbecue sauce. Stir to combine. Cook on low for 4 hours, on high for 2, or until heated throughout. Serve with toothpicks right out of the slow cooker.

The Verdict

These are great Smokies. The flavor is a bit more sophisticated than the Grape Jelly and Chili Sauce Little Smokies (page 25), and tastes better than just using plain barbecue sauce. You can also add $^{1}/_{2}$ teaspoon dried red chile flakes to the pot for a spicy flavor.

DOUBLE ARTICHOKE DIP

serves 8

The Ingredients

1 (14-ounce) can artichoke hearts, rinsed, drained, and chopped
1 (6.5-ounce) jar marinated artichoke hearts, drained and chopped
1 (4-ounce) can chopped green chiles (mild or hot, your choice)
¼ cup mayonnaise
3 cups shredded cheddar cheese
bread cubes, crackers, or tortilla chips for serving

The Directions

Use a 2-quart slow cooker. Drain the two containers of artichokes, and chop the hearts coarsely with a knife. Put into the slow cooker with the chiles. Stir in the mayonnaise and shredded cheese. Cover and cook on low for 3 to 4 hours, or on high for about 2 hours. Stir really well, and serve with bread cubes, crackers, or tortilla chips.

The Verdict

Artichoke dip is always a hit at parties, and I really like how artichoke-y this tastes. Sometimes all you can taste is the mayonnaise or cream cheese, but in this dip the artichoke is the key player. I like using hot chiles, but that makes it too spicy for my kids to enjoy. Maybe that's why I like it like that . . . ?

FRUIT AND HORSERADISH CREAM CHEESE SPREAD

serves 8

The Ingredients

    1 (8-ounce) package cream cheese
    1 tablespoon prepared horseradish
    $1/3$ cup apricot preserves
    1 (1-ounce) box dried unsweetened cranberries ($1/4$ cup)
    crackers or salted corn tortilla chips for serving

The Directions

Use a 2-quart slow cooker. Unwrap the cream cheese and put it into the cooker. Top with the horseradish and preserves. Pour in the dried cranberries. Cover and cook on low for 2 to 3 hours, or on high for 1 to 2 hours. Serve warm with your favorite crackers or salted corn tortilla chips.

The Verdict

This tastes great, even though the ingredient list sounds a bit odd. Adam, the girls, my grandma, and I all really liked it a lot. Next time you're in a dip rut, give this a try.

ORANGE-GLAZED MEATBALLS

serves 5

The Ingredients

20 frozen meatballs (Coleman Natural® and Aidells® make a gluten-free variety)
1 (12-ounce) jar orange marmalade
1/4 cup orange juice
3 green onions, sliced
1 jalapeño pepper

The Directions

Use a 4-quart slow cooker. Put the frozen meatballs into the bottom of your slow cooker. Add the marmalade, orange juice, and sliced green onions. Toss the meatballs with a large spoon to cover with the sauce. Throw in a washed whole jalapeño pepper. Cover and cook on low for 5 hours, or until the meatballs have heated through. Serve with toothpicks as an appetizer.

The Verdict

These are sweet meatballs with an infused smoky spiced flavor thanks to the jalapeño. They make a great appetizer, and are a nice change from traditional party meatballs in barbecue sauce. I like cooking with jalapeños this way. Even when wearing gloves, I somehow find a way to sting my fingers when chopping jalapeños. Leaving them whole in the pot allows the spicy flavor to steam out without injury.

WASABI ALMONDS

serves 10

The Ingredients

1 egg white
1 tablespoon water
1 tablespoon gluten-free soy sauce
1 pound raw almonds
2 teaspoons cornstarch
2 tablespoons wasabi powder
1 teaspoon kosher salt

The Directions

Use a 2-quart slow cooker. Mix the egg white, water, and soy sauce in a small bowl until foamy. Toss the almonds with this liquid. Combine the cornstarch, wasabi powder, and salt in a plastic zippered freezer bag. Drain any remaining liquid from the almonds and pour the almonds into the bag. Close tightly and shake to coat the almonds with the powder. Dump the bag contents into your slow cooker and cover. Cook on low for 2 to 4 hours, or until toasty. Let the almonds dry completely on a length of aluminum foil or parchment paper spread out on the kitchen table or kitchen countertop. Store leftovers in an airtight container in the refrigerator.

The Verdict

What a terrific snack! The almonds toast nicely in the slow cooker (if a few on the edge brown too much, that's okay, that's what makes them homemade!), and the combo of soy sauce and wasabi powder can't be beat. I didn't find these nuts spicy at all. If you'd prefer a stronger flavor, increase the wasabi measurement.

My regular neighborhood grocery store sells tiny cans of wasabi powder in the Asian cooking aisle for $3.99 a can. If you can't find this spice locally, you can purchase it online (I love shopping in my jammies!).

SOUPS & STEWS

Ethiopian Chicken Stew 126

Hungarian Beef Stew 127

Lean, Mean & Green Tortilla Soup 128

Manhattan Clam Chowder 129

Minestrone Soup 130

Spinach Bisque 131

Turkey Stew 132

Vegetarian Tortilla Soup 134

Yellow Split Pea Soup with Smoked Paprika 136

ETHIOPIAN CHICKEN STEW

serves 8

The Ingredients

1 (14.5-ounce) can diced tomatoes, undrained
1½ pounds boneless, skinless chicken thighs
¼ cup fresh lemon juice
2 tablespoons butter
3 large onions, diced (or 3 tablespoons dried minced onion flakes)
1 teaspoon ground ginger
1 tablespoon paprika
1 teaspoon cayenne pepper, more to taste
½ teaspoon black pepper
1 teaspoon ground turmeric
2 cups water
8 hard-boiled eggs (to add later)

The Directions

Use a 6-quart slow cooker. Empty the contents of the canned tomatoes into your slow cooker. Put in the chicken thighs and lemon juice. Add a pat of butter, diced onion, and all the spices. Pour in the water. Cover and cook on low for 6 to 8 hours, high for 4 to 5 hours, or until the onions are soft and translucent. Ladle into bowls with a peeled but intact hard-boiled egg.

The Verdict

The inspiration for this stew comes from Mary Ostyn, who writes at OwlHaven.net and is the author of *Family Feasts for $75 a Week*. Mary writes that this spicy stew is called Doro Wat, and is traditionally served in Ethiopia at Christmastime. She says to make it authentic, you should use 1 tablespoon of cayenne pepper but to begin with 1 teaspoon. This amount was plenty spicy for me. I really liked taking a bit of hard-boiled egg in each bite.

HUNGARIAN BEEF STEW

serves 6

The Ingredients

3 pounds beef stew meat

combine in a food processor or blender:
2 green bell peppers, seeded
2 onions, peeled
2 garlic cloves, peeled
1 (6-ounce) can tomato paste
2 teaspoons kosher salt
1 teaspoon paprika
1 teaspoon black pepper
1/2 cup water

The Directions

Use a 6-quart slow cooker. Put the meat into your slow cooker. Combine all the other ingredients in a food processor or blender, and pulse until mixed well and a sauce forms. Pour the sauce over the meat. That's it! Cover and cook on low for 8 to 10 hours, or until the meat chunks are super tender and can be cut easily with a spoon.

The Verdict

Ayalla, who writes at saltandpaprika.com, sent me this recipe. She serves it to her family with homemade biscuits and a spinach salad. I loved how easy this stew was to make, and smiled watching my kids eat it up, bell peppers and all. This is a great technique to "sneak" in extra vegetables.

LEAN, MEAN & GREEN TORTILLA SOUP

serves 6 to 8

The Ingredients

4 boneless, skinless chicken thighs
6 cups chicken broth
1 (16-ounce) bag frozen corn
1 (14-ounce) jar prepared salsa verde (I'd go for mild; you can always add more spice at the table)
1 tablespoon ground cumin
6 tablespoons sour cream (to add before serving)
crushed tortilla chips, avocado slices, and cilantro as garnish (optional)

The Directions

Use a 6-quart slow cooker. Place the chicken into the bottom of your slow cooker insert. Stir in the chicken broth, corn, salsa verde, and cumin. Cover and cook on low for 6 to 8 hours, or on high for about 4 hours. Shred the chicken using two large forks before serving. Ladle into bowls with a dollop of sour cream in each bowl, and top with crushed tortilla chips, avocado, and cilantro, if you'd like.

The Verdict

This recipe comes from Sara W., who adapted Rachael Ray's Mean Green Tortilla Soup to work in the slow cooker. We both decided to use salsa verde instead of blending tomatillos (which can be quite expensive in some areas), and the result is fantastic. Sara likes the "tequila lime" salsa verde—yum!

MANHATTAN CLAM CHOWDER

serves 4

The Ingredients

2 (6.5-ounce) cans clams (and juice)
1 (14.5-ounce) can Italian-seasoned diced tomatoes (and juice)
1 cup chopped celery
1 cup chopped green bell pepper
½ cup chopped carrot
2 cups finely diced peeled potato
¼ teaspoon red cayenne pepper
1 cup chicken broth

The Directions

Use a 4-quart slow cooker. Put the clams and tomatoes in the cooker. Add the chopped vegetables and red pepper. Pour in the chicken broth. Cover and cook on low for 6 to 8 hours, or until the potatoes are quite tender.

The Verdict

This was great! My kids really liked this a lot. They had never tried red clam chowder before, and were a bit hesitant at first. I served it with a batch of drop biscuits (made from a gluten-free baking mix), but if we weren't gluten-free, I'd opt for a nice crusty sourdough roll.

MINESTRONE SOUP

serves 6

The Ingredients

8 cups beef broth
1 (14.5-ounce) can diced tomatoes (whole can)
1 cup dry pinto, black, or lima beans, rinsed in hot water
1 cup chopped carrots
1 cup sliced celery
1 tablespoon dried minced onion (or 1 small onion, diced)
1 tablespoon Italian seasoning
1 (10-ounce) package frozen chopped spinach, thawed and drained
1/2 cup dried pasta (to add later, I used brown rice fusilli)
Parmesan cheese for garnish

The Directions

Use a 6-quart slow cooker. Pour the broth and tomatoes into your slow cooker. Add the dried beans. I didn't soak my beans ahead of time since there was so much liquid in the pot, but if you live in a high-altitude area, you should soak them overnight or boil on the stove for 10 minutes.

Add the vegetables, Italian seasoning, and drained spinach. Cover and cook on low for 8 to 10 hours, or until the vegetables and beans are bite-tender. Stir in the raw pasta and cook on high for 20 to 30 minutes, or until the pasta is fully cooked. Serve in bowls with grated Parmesan cheese.

The Verdict

My kids loved their soup, and both big girls ate two bowls. I served our minestrone with mini corn muffins made from a gluten-free mix. This soup freezes and reheats quite well. If you decide to use dry red beans in this soup, remember to boil them for at least 10 minutes before adding to the cooker to kill a possible toxin that occurs naturally in red beans.

SPINACH BISQUE

serves 8

The Ingredients

1 (10-ounce) package frozen chopped spinach, thawed and drained
1/2 cup chopped onion
1/4 cup butter, melted
1/4 cup all-purpose flour (I used a gluten-free baking mix)
2 cups low-fat milk
1 cup water
1/2 teaspoon kosher salt
1/4 teaspoon ground nutmeg
1 (16-ounce) package Velveeta®, cubed

The Directions

Use a 4-quart slow cooker. Put the spinach into the bottom of your slow cooker. Add the chopped onion. In a bowl, whisk together the melted butter and flour to form a roux. Slowly add the milk and water to the bowl. Stir in the salt and nutmeg. Pour the milk mixture into the slow cooker. Add the Velveeta® cubes. Cover and cook on low for 5 to 6 hours, or until the onions are tender and translucent. Stir well before serving in soup bowls.

The Verdict

This is a creamy and decadent soup that will warm you up on a cold day. I loved it and so did my grandma. The kids loved this cheesy soup and each ate a big bowlful. It's difficult not to love anything made with Velveeta®!

TURKEY STEW

serves 8

The Ingredients

There are two parts here. The first part is to make broth with your leftover turkey carcass. If you don't have a carcass on hand and would still like to make this soup, jump to the next step and use 8 cups chicken broth and 2 to 3 cups chopped turkey.

FOR BROTH

turkey carcass or rib cage bone sets from 2 turkey breasts

9 cups water

2 tablespoons gluten-free granulated chicken bouillon

2 tablespoons balsamic vinegar

1 large onion, finely diced, OR 1 tablespoon dried onion flakes

Put all the ingredients into a 6-quart slow cooker. Cook on low overnight, or for about 8 hours. Unplug and remove the stoneware from the cooking element. Uncover and let cool. When cool enough to "go fishing," remove all the bones from the broth, leaving the meat in the pot.

Note: If your slow cooker releases a bunch of steam and condensation while cooking, put a layer of foil or parchment paper down over the top, then put the lid on so you don't lose your cooking liquid.

FOR STEW

2 cups peeled and diced sweet potato

1 (28-ounce) can diced or stewed Italian-style tomatoes

1 teaspoon dried oregano

1 teaspoon ground coriander

1 tablespoon chili powder

1 (15-ounce) can corn and juice

4 garlic cloves, chopped, or 1 teaspoon dried garlic powder

MORE MAKE IT FAST, COOK IT SLOW

The Directions

Use a 6-quart slow cooker. Throw everything into the pot and cook on low for 6 to 7 hours, or until the sweet potatoes have reached the desired tenderness and the flavors have melded.

The Verdict

We all really liked this a lot. The girls were slow to warm up because they thought the name "turkey stew" was weird and didn't like that the broth wasn't clear, but I didn't offer them anything else to eat. When they finally tasted it, they happily finished their bowls. This stew does not have any spicy taste, just lots of flavor. It's been very well received by my Web site readers.

VEGETARIAN TORTILLA SOUP

serves 8

The Ingredients

1 cup dry pinto beans, soaked overnight
1 (15-ounce) can fire-roasted tomatoes
1 medium yellow onion, diced
3 garlic cloves, minced
1/2 teaspoon dried oregano
1/4 teaspoon chipotle chile powder
1/2 teaspoon smoked paprika
1/2 teaspoon kosher salt
4 cups vegetable broth
4 cups water
4 whole serrano chiles
1 to 2 handfuls baby spinach (optional)
shredded cheddar cheese and sour cream (optional garnishes)

The Directions

Use a 6-quart slow cooker. Put the presoaked and drained beans into the slow cooker. If you don't have time to soak the beans, you can boil them rapidly on the stove for 10 minutes, then let them sit in the hot water for 1 hour before draining and using in the slow cooker.

Add the entire can of tomatoes, the onion, and garlic. Follow with all the spices, broth, and water. Wash the serrano chiles and float them on top of the soup—do not cut. Cover and cook on low for 8 to 10 hours, or on high for 4 to 5 hours. Remove the chiles before serving (unless you're much braver than I am). If desired, drop a handful of baby spinach into the pot and stir to wilt. Garnish with shredded cheddar cheese and/or sour cream.

The Verdict

There is some heat to this soup. I found my nose running a bit, but my tongue was never uncomfortable. I put the end of a bag of Tostitos® into the kids' servings, but it was still too spicy for them. Adam and I happily ate the leftovers for lunch. Stretch the leftovers by stirring in already-cooked rice or pasta when reheated.

YELLOW SPLIT PEA SOUP WITH SMOKED PAPRIKA

serves 4

The Ingredients

1 cup yellow split peas
1 quart (4 cups) chicken broth
2 garlic cloves, minced
1 onion, peeled and finely diced
$\frac{1}{2}$ teaspoon smoked paprika
$\frac{1}{4}$ teaspoon kosher salt

The Directions

Use a 4-quart slow cooker. Rinse the split peas in hot water and add to the slow cooker. Pour in the broth, and stir in the garlic and onion. Add the smoked paprika and salt. Cover and cook on low for 6 to 8 hours, 4 to 5 hours on high, or until the split peas have softened and soaked up the broth. Use a handheld stick blender to puree the peas into a creamy soup.

The Verdict

This soup is a great starter to a meat-and-potatoes meal or to enjoy as a light lunch. My mother-in-law took this soup home and happily ate it for lunch for three days. Smoked paprika is a great spice—I use the McCormick® brand, and can find it at my neighborhood Safeway.

BEANS

Chicken Enchilada Chili *138*

Indian Spiced Lentils with Chicken *139*

Pepperoni Pizza Chili *141*

Pineapple Baked Beans *142*

Sloppy Lentils *143*

Smoked Sausage and Bean Stew *144*

CHICKEN ENCHILADA CHILI

serves 6

The Ingredients

1½ cups prepared enchilada sauce (read labels carefully if avoiding gluten)
2 (14.5-ounce) cans tomatoes with seasoning (your choice: I had garlic and olive oil on hand)
2 (15-ounce) cans pinto or kidney beans with juice (or 1 cup dry pinto beans, soaked overnight)
2 celery stalks, chopped
1 onion, diced, or 1 tablespoon dried minced onion flakes
1 to 2 teaspoons chili powder
1 teaspoon ground cumin
1½ pounds chicken (thighs, legs, breasts—your choice)
shredded cheddar cheese and sour cream for serving (optional)

The Directions

Use a 6-quart slow cooker. Pour the enchilada sauce and tomatoes into the bottom of the removable stoneware insert. Add the beans, celery, onion, and spices, and stir to combine. Place the chicken on top.

Cover and cook on low for 7 to 8 hours, or until the flavors have combined. If you are using dry beans, you may need to cook longer to fully soften the beans. If your chicken has bones, fish the bones out before serving. Serve with shredded cheddar cheese and a dollop of sour cream, if desired.

The Verdict

Oh, I LOVED this chili! And I loved it even more that Adam and the kids loved it, and that the baby doesn't seem to mind when I eat beans. I made an afternoon snack of nachos with some of the leftovers. Divine. This is such a fun twist on traditional chili, and I absolutely adored every last drop. There is definitely a bit of heat in the sauce—if your family doesn't like much heat, start with 1 teaspoon chili powder. You can always add more later. Like many soups, stews, and chilis, the leftovers are even better than the original!

INDIAN SPICED LENTILS WITH CHICKEN

serves 4

The Ingredients

2 cups brown lentils

3 cups chicken broth

3 cups water

1 small yellow onion, diced

1 cup diced celery

1 teaspoon ground cumin

1/2 teaspoon ground coriander

1 teaspoon kosher salt

1/2 teaspoon dry mustard

1/2 teaspoon turmeric

4 garlic cloves, chopped

1 tablespoon dried parsley (or 1/4 cup finely chopped fresh)

1 (4-ounce) can diced chiles (hot or mild, your choice)–no need to drain

2 large boneless chicken breast halves

basmati rice, corn tortillas, or naan wedges for serving

The Directions

Use a 4-quart slow cooker. Rinse the lentils under cold water until it runs clear. Dump into your slow cooker. Add the broth, water, onion, and celery. Add all the spices, the garlic, parsley, and chiles. Stir to combine.

Lay 2 large-ish chicken breast halves on top of the assembled food. My breast halves were frozen solid when I put them in.

Cover and cook on low for about 7 hours, or on high for about 4 hours. Before serving, chop the

(CONTINUED)

chicken into bite-size pieces, and stir back in. Serve over basmati rice with corn tortillas or naan wedges (these are not gluten-free) as scoopers.

The Verdict

I started this recipe thinking I'd get a soup, but I didn't. Instead I got a superbly spiced lentil dish that the whole family enjoyed. Adam added a bit of spice to his with some red chile flakes, but I abstained because I was worried about getting pregnancy heartburn. I heated the leftovers up for lunch, and my almost-five-year-old and her friend happily ate them.

PEPPERONI PIZZA CHILI

serves 6

The Ingredients

1 pound lean ground beef, browned and drained
1 (15-ounce) can kidney beans, undrained
1 (14-ounce) jar pizza sauce
1 (14.5-ounce) can Italian stewed tomatoes
1 green bell pepper, seeded and diced
1 teaspoon Italian seasoning
25 pepperoni pieces
1 cup water
shredded mozzarella cheese for serving (optional, although not optional in our house!)

The Directions

Use a 6-quart slow cooker. Brown the beef in a large skillet on the stovetop until it is no longer pink, and drain well. Scrape the meat into slow cooker insert. Add the beans, pizza sauce, and tomatoes. Add the diced bell pepper, then stir in the Italian seasoning and pepperoni (I didn't chop the pepperoni, but you can if you'd prefer smaller pieces). Pour in the water. Cover and cook on low for 8 hours, or on high for about 4 hours. Your chili is done when the green peppers have softened completely and the flavors have melded. Serve with a sprinkling of mozzarella cheese, if desired.

The Verdict

Liquid pizza: Life couldn't get any better. If you're watching your carb intake, this will satisfy every one of your pizza cravings without a drop of guilt.

PINEAPPLE BAKED BEANS

serves 12

The Ingredients

2 pounds kielbasa sausage, sliced
1 onion, peeled and diced
1 (16-ounce) can baked beans
1 (16-ounce) can kidney beans, drained and rinsed
1 (15-ounce) can pinto beans, drained and rinsed
1 (15-ounce) can butter beans, drained and rinsed
1 (8-ounce) can pineapple chunks, drained
1 tart apple, peeled and shredded
1/2 cup ketchup
1/2 cup molasses
shredded sharp cheddar cheese as garnish (optional)

The Directions

Use a 6-quart slow cooker. Put the sliced kielbasa into the slow cooker. Top with the onion and all the beans. Add the pineapple chunks and shredded apple. Stir in the ketchup and molasses. Cover and cook on low for 8 to 9 hours. Serve with shredded cheddar cheese, if desired.

The Verdict

This is an excellent take-along to a potluck event. It serves an awful lot of people, and is both sweet and savory—a winning combination. I shared containers of this with my whole family, and my grandma reported back that leftovers freeze and reheat quite well.

SLOPPY LENTILS

serves 8

The Ingredients

    2 cups lentils
    1 large onion, diced
    2 celery stalks, diced
    1 green bell pepper, seeded and diced
    $1/2$ teaspoon dried basil
    $1/2$ teaspoon garlic powder
    1 teaspoon chili powder
    1 tablespoon gluten-free soy sauce
    $1^{1}/2$ teaspoons prepared mustard (and more to taste, after cooking)
    2 (12-ounce) cans tomato paste
    4 empty tomato paste cans water
    8 hamburger buns (or rice cakes, or serve over rice)

The Directions

Use a 4-quart slow cooker. Sort the lentils and rinse in hot water. Dump into the slow cooker. Add the onion, celery, and bell pepper. Add the spices, soy sauce, and mustard. Add the contents of the tomato paste cans, then add 4 cans of water. Stir to combine the ingredients. Cover and cook on low for 8 hours, or until the lentils have softened nicely. Stir well and taste. If desired, squeeze in a bit more mustard. Serve on hamburger buns, rice cakes, or over brown or white rice.

The Verdict

I really liked this play on traditional Sloppy Joes! This recipe came from one of my readers, Trish, who makes it often for her family. Lentils are full of fiber, and are an easy bean to cook in the slow cooker—no soaking required.

SMOKED SAUSAGE AND BEAN STEW

serves 6

The Ingredients

1 pound smoked sausage, casings removed, crumbled

1 cup chopped carrot

1 cup chopped celery

2 brown potatoes, diced (no need to peel)

½ cup dry lima beans (no need to presoak lima beans)

1 tablespoon A-1® sauce (the secret ingredient!)

4 cups beef broth

The Directions

Use a 6-quart slow cooker. Remove casings from sausage, and put into slow cooker. Add the vegetables and lima beans. Pour in the A-1® sauce and beef broth. Cover and cook on low for 8 to 10 hours, or until the beans and carrot have reached the desired tenderness.

The Verdict

The flavor from this stew comes directly from the sausage and a bit of tang from the A-1 sauce. If you use spicy sausage, you'll end up with a spicy stew. The beans grow quite a lot while cooking—using ½ cup is plenty.

SIDE DISHES

RICE

Best Brussels Sprouts *146*

Carrot Pudding *147*

Cauliflower Gratin *148*

Dill Baby Carrots *149*

Orange-Glazed Beets *150*

Pizza Potatoes *151*

BEST BRUSSELS SPROUTS

serves 6

The Ingredients

1 pound brussels sprouts
3 tablespoons butter
1 tablespoon Dijon mustard
1/4 teaspoon kosher salt
1/4 teaspoon pepper
1/4 cup water

The Directions

Use a 2-quart slow cooker. Wash and trim the ends off of each Brussels sprout. Cut each sprout in half, and toss into the slow cooker. Add the butter, mustard, salt, pepper, and water. Cover and cook on low for 4 to 5 hours, or on high for 2 to 3 hours. Stir to distribute the sauce before serving.

The Verdict

My eight-year-old's favorite vegetable is brussels sprouts. She must have been absent in school the day her classmates announced that liking brussels sprouts at a young age is a tiny bit odd. She will gladly make an entire meal out of these sprouts, and we proudly cheer her on. Adam and I really like the savory component the Dijon mustard provides. If you aren't normally a fan of this vegetable, you might find yourself won over by this ingredient combination.

CARROT PUDDING

serves 10

The Ingredients

    4 cups grated carrots
    1 small onion, grated
    1 cup heavy cream
    1 egg, beaten
    2 teaspoons kosher salt
    1 teaspoon ground nutmeg
    1 tablespoon sugar

The Directions

Use a 4-quart slow cooker. Put the grated carrots and onion into your slow cooker. In a mixing bowl, combine the cream, egg, salt, nutmeg, and sugar. Pour the mixture into your slow cooker, and stir to mix with the grated carrots and onion. Cover and cook on low for 4 to 5 hours, or on high for 2 to 3 hours. When the carrots are tender, blend with a handheld stick blender or in a traditional blender to create a pudding-like consistency. Serve alongside meat and potatoes.

The Verdict

This is a very heavy side dish—just a small amount is plenty. It pairs really well with a juicy steak and a baked potato. I've had similar carrot dishes in fancy restaurants, and love how simple and inexpensive it is to make at home in the slow cooker.

CAULIFLOWER GRATIN

serves 4 to 6

The Ingredients

1 head cauliflower
4 tablespoons butter, melted
3 tablespoons all-purpose flour (I used Pamela's Baking Mix)
2 cups heavy cream or half-and-half
1 teaspoon kosher salt
$\frac{1}{2}$ teaspoon black pepper
$\frac{1}{2}$ teaspoon ground nutmeg
1 cup shredded Swiss or Gruyère cheese

The Directions

Use a 4-quart slow cooker. Wash and separate the cauliflower florets. Place into the bottom of the slow cooker. In a mixing bowl, whisk together the melted butter and flour to make a roux. Slowly whisk in the cream. Add the spices and shredded cheese. Pour the milky cheese mixture on top of the cauliflower. Cover and cook on low for 5 to 6 hours, or until lightly browned on top and the cauliflower reaches the desired tenderness.

The Verdict

If you've got fussy people in the house who insist they don't like cauliflower, this recipe will win them over. The finished result is gooey and delicious. I like the way the cheese gets a bit crusty along the edges—it's my favorite part.

DILL BABY CARROTS

serves 4

The Ingredients

1 (16-ounce) package baby carrots
2 tablespoons butter
1 teaspoon dried dill
1 tablespoon lemon juice
$\frac{1}{2}$ teaspoon kosher salt
$\frac{1}{4}$ teaspoon pepper

The Directions

Use a 2-quart slow cooker. Wash the baby carrots (even though the package says prewashed, I wash them because I promised my dad I would), and dump into the slow cooker. Add the butter, dill, lemon juice, salt, and pepper. Toss to coat. Cover and cook on low for 5 hours, or on high for 2 to 3 hours. I like my carrots al dente.

The Verdict

This is a great accompaniment to a roasted chicken or pot roast. The lemon and dill combination is superb with the sweetness of the cooked carrots. Yum.

ORANGE-GLAZED BEETS

serves 6

The Ingredients

4 medium beets, peeled and sliced in $\frac{1}{4}$-inch slices
$\frac{1}{4}$ cup butter
1 tablespoon brown sugar
$\frac{1}{4}$ teaspoon orange zest
$\frac{1}{4}$ cup orange juice

The Directions

Use a 4-quart slow cooker. Carefully (and wearing old clothes, beets stain!) peel and slice the beets, and place into the stoneware insert. Add the butter, brown sugar, orange zest, and orange juice. Toss the beets with spoons to distribute the sugar. The butter will still be in a clump, and that's okay. Cover and cook on low for 5 hours, or on high for 2 to 3 hours. Serve when the beets have reached the desired tenderness.

The Verdict

I am not a beet person, and won't go out of my way to eat them on a regular basis. I don't mind the flavor as much as I mind the color and texture. Adam really enjoys them, though, so I take one for the team and make them every so often. He really likes them prepared like this, and pretty much ate them all by himself. If you have a white countertop or sink, be careful to not get beet juice everywhere because it stains.

PIZZA POTATOES

serves 6 to 8

The Ingredients

4 to 6 large russet or Idaho potatoes
1 small onion, diced
2 ounces pepperoni slices, quartered
1 (14-ounce) jar pizza sauce
2 cups shredded mozzarella cheese

The Directions

Use a 4-quart slow cooker. Wash the potatoes well and cut into 1-inch chunks. I didn't peel them. Put the potatoes, onion, and pepperoni into the slow cooker. Pour in the pizza sauce and add the cheese. Stir with a wooden spoon to combine the ingredients. Cover and cook on low for 6 hours, or on high for about 3 hours. The potatoes should be bite-tender when served.

The Verdict

The next time you're asked for a side dish at a potluck and are stumped on what to bring, try this potato recipe—it's a crowd pleaser. I get excited when it's buy-one/get-one-free day on five-pound bags of potatoes. Because of this, I sometimes end up with way too many potatoes in the house, and struggle to make my way through them before they begin to sprout. This is a great change of pace from mashed or baked potatoes.

VEGETARIAN MAIN COURSES

Artichoke Pasta *153*

Pesto Lasagna *154*

Teriyaki Portobello Mushrooms *155*

ARTICHOKE PASTA

serves 4

The Ingredients

3 (14.5-ounce) cans Italian tomatoes (do not drain)
2 (14-ounce) cans artichoke hearts in water, drained and lightly chopped
6 garlic cloves, minced
$\frac{1}{2}$ cup pimiento-stuffed olives
$\frac{1}{2}$ cup heavy whipping cream (to add later)
1 pound pasta, cooked (I used brown rice penne)

The Directions

Use a 6-quart slow cooker. Pour the tomatoes into your slow cooker. Lightly chop drained artichoke hearts and add to the pot. Add the garlic and olives. Cover and cook on low for 4 to 5 hours. Stir in the heavy cream and hot, freshly cooked pasta, and serve.

The Verdict

This tastes like a dish you'd expect to be served in a restaurant. Even though only a small amount of olives are in the sauce, they really do a lot to make it magnificent. The next time you invite company over for a pasta dinner, surprise them with this sauce. It also makes the house smell fantastic!

PESTO LASAGNA

serves 8

The Ingredients

1 (26-ounce) jar prepared pasta sauce
1 (10-ounce) box lasagna noodles (I used brown rice noodles)
1 (11-ounce) container pesto
1 (15-ounce) container ricotta cheese
1 (12-ounce) bag baby spinach
1 cup grated Parmesan cheese
16 ounces mozzarella cheese, sliced
1/4 cup water

The Directions

Use a 4-quart slow cooker. Put 1/4 cup or so of pasta sauce into the bottom of a slow cooker insert. Top the sauce with a layer of uncooked lasagna noodles (you will have to break the noodles to make them fit nicely). Smear a bit of pesto and ricotta cheese onto the noodles. Add a handful or two of baby spinach, and top with a layer of Parmesan and mozzarella cheeses. Repeat the layers, starting with the pasta sauce, until you've run out of ingredients or your insert is full (push down to squish the spinach!). Put the water into the empty pasta sauce jar and shake. Pour the saucy liquid evenly over the top. Cover and cook on low for 6 hours, or on high for 3 to 4 hours. The top layer will brown and begin to pull away from the sides. Uncover and let sit for 10 to 15 minutes before serving.

The Verdict

We loved this so much! This was an "accidental" recipe. Adam brought home two containers of pesto from the store instead of the one I asked for, and I didn't want it to go bad. I had already planned on making traditional lasagna and had the other ingredients in the house. Although there isn't a drop of meat, this was a very filling lasagna, and a new favorite.

TERIYAKI PORTOBELLO MUSHROOMS

serves 4

The Ingredients

1 tablespoon olive oil
1 pound portobello mushrooms, stems removed
2 tablespoons brown sugar
2 tablespoons gluten-free soy sauce
½ teaspoon dry mustard
½ teaspoon ground ginger

The Directions

Use a 2-quart slow cooker. Put the olive oil into the bottom of your slow cooker and smear it around. After washing the mushrooms, remove and discard the stems, and cut the mushrooms into thirds. Place them into the cooker. Add the brown sugar, soy sauce, mustard, and ginger. Toss the mushrooms with spoons (I used my hands) until the flavorings are evenly distributed. Cover and cook on low for 6 hours, or on high for about 3.

The Verdict

Portobello mushrooms are a great meat substitute. I love how thick and hearty they are, and how sturdy they remain, even when slow cooked. The teriyaki flavor permeates the mushrooms, and they taste great over rice, or either hot or cold in a sandwich. My girls aren't fans—my eldest said the texture was "like eating a snail," which kept her younger sister from giving it a try.

FISH

Ginger Tilapia with Bok Choy *157*

Greek Fish in Foil *158*

Herb, the Catfish *159*

Orange and Honey Tilapia *160*

Salmon Loaf *161*

GINGER TILAPIA WITH BOK CHOY

serves 2 to 4

The Ingredients

aluminum foil
2 tilapia fillets
1 teaspoon dried ginger
$1/2$ teaspoon crushed red pepper flakes
1 tablespoon gluten-free soy sauce
2 green onions, sliced
2 bunches bok choy, coarsely chopped

The Directions

Use a 6-quart slow cooker. Lay a length of foil out on your kitchen countertop. Place the fish fillets in the center, sprinkle the ginger and red peper flakes onto the fish, and top with the soy sauce. Add the green onions and bok choy. Fold the foil over and crimp the edges to make a packet. Place the packet in the bottom of your slow cooker (do not add water). Cover and cook on high for 2 hours, or until the fish flakes easily with a fork.

The Verdict

We eat a lot of tilapia in our house, and I'm happy to have another recipe to add to the rotation. The fish gets nicely flavored and steamed in the foil packets. This was more than enough food to feed my family of four fish eaters (the baby was only six weeks old when I made this!), but you might need to add an additional fish fillet if you have bigger eaters in the house.

GREEK FISH IN FOIL

serves 2

The Ingredients
aluminum foil
2 firm white fish fillets (I use tilapia)
1 small fennel bulb, thinly sliced
1 tomato, thinly sliced
1 red onion, sliced in rings
1 teaspoon dried dill
1 lime, juiced
salt and pepper to taste

The Directions
Use a 6-quart slow cooker. Lay out a length of foil onto your kitchen countertop and place the fish fillets in the center. Top the fish with the slices of fennel, tomato, and onion. Sprinkle on the dill and lime juice. Fold the foil over and crimp the edges to make a packet. Put the packet into an empty slow cooker (do not add water). Cover and cook on high for 2 hours, or until the fish flakes easily with a fork. Season to taste with salt and pepper.

The Verdict
Adam and I found the fennel and tomato a great combination with the dill and lime. The tilapia cooked perfectly in the foil packet—just like always.

HERB, THE CATFISH

serves 4

The Ingredients

aluminum foil
4 catfish fillets
$\frac{1}{2}$ teaspoon dried basil
$\frac{1}{2}$ teaspoon dried thyme
$\frac{1}{2}$ teaspoon dried dill
2 lemons (1 juiced, 1 sliced in thin rings)

The Directions

Use a 6-quart slow cooker. Lay a length of foil out on your kitchen countertop and place the fish fillets in the center. Sprinkle the spices directly onto the fish, and squeeze the juice of 1 lemon all over. Lay the lemon slices on the fish, fold the foil over, and crimp the edges to form a packet. Place the packet into the bottom of your slow cooker (do not add water). Cover and cook on high for 2 hours, or until the fish flakes easily with a fork.

The Verdict

I was on the phone when my eight-year-old daughter asked me what we were having for dinner. I wrote "herb catfish" on the kitchen chalkboard, and she took off running through the house to inform her younger sister that we were going to eat a catfish named Herb. (P.S. Herb tasted delicious!)

ORANGE AND HONEY TILAPIA

serves 4

The Ingredients

aluminum foil
4 tilapia fillets
2 tablespoons balsamic vinegar
1 tablespoon honey
1 (10-ounce) can mandarin oranges, drained
salt and pepper to taste

The Directions

Use a 6-quart slow cooker. Lay a length of foil out on the countertop and place the fish fillets in the center. Dribble the balsamic vinegar and honey over the top of the fish, and pour on the drained mandarin oranges (my kids like to drink the juice). Fold the foil over the fish, and crimp the sides to make a fully enclosed packet. Put into your slow cooker (do not add water) and cover. Cook on high for 2 hours, or until the fish flakes easily with a fork. Add salt and pepper at the table.

The Verdict

When I was growing up, I spent my after-school hours at my grandparents' house. My grandpa liked to tease that mandarin oranges were actually tiny little boneless goldfish. This means that in my head, this fish dish is seasoned with baby goldfish. I know this sounds terribly odd—but this thought evokes such fond memories I don't ever want to shake it.

SALMON LOAF

serves 4

The Ingredients

aluminum foil strips
1 (14.75-ounce) can salmon, drained and deboned
2 cups toast crumbs (I used brown rice bread)
1 teaspoon garlic powder
1/2 teaspoon black pepper
1 tablespoon dried parsley
1/2 teaspoon dry mustard
1/4 cup butter, melted
1/2 cup grated Parmesan cheese
2 eggs, lightly beaten
1 cup chicken broth

The Directions

Use a 2 quart slow cooker. Tear out four 6-inch lengths of foil. Fold each length into a 1-inch-wide strip. Place two strips of foil in the bottom of the stoneware insert lengthwise and the other two crossing these (you are going to use the foil strips to lift the cooked loaf out of the slow cooker). In a mixing bowl, combine the canned salmon, toast crumbs, and spices. Pour in the melted butter and Parmesan cheese. Stir in the eggs and form the mix into a rounded blob. Put this mixture (it should resemble a wet meatloaf) into the middle of the crossed foil strips at the bottom of your slow cooker. Pour the chicken broth evenly over the top. Cover and cook on low for 4 to 6 hours, or on high for 2 to 3 hours. Use the foil strips to carefully lift the loaf out of the pot.

(CONTINUED)

The Verdict

Ah! This is so good! I was hesitant to give it a try—the recipe was e-mailed to me a few times from several readers, but I was concerned that I wouldn't like it. Not only did I enjoy this, so did the kids. Although you can eat this as a full meal, I served it on rice cakes as a midmorning snack.

POULTRY

Chicken Cacciatore   *164*

Chicken with Apricots and Dates   *165*

Green Pepper Chicken   *166*

Herb Garden Chicken   *168*

Herb-Roasted Chicken with Summer Tomatoes   *169*

Japanese Takeout Turkey   *171*

Not-So-Sloppy Joes   *173*

Pesto Chicken and Sweet Potatoes Layered Dinner   *174*

Pizza Chicken   *176*

CHICKEN CACCIATORE

serves 6

The Ingredients

1 pound boneless, skinless chicken thighs
1 yellow onion, peeled and sliced in rings
1 green or red bell pepper, seeded and sliced
1 cup chopped celery
8 ounces sliced mushrooms
4 garlic cloves, chopped
1 (28-ounce) can crushed tomatoes
1 tablespoon Italian seasoning
2 tablespoons paprika
1/4 teaspoon pepper
Hot pasta for serving

The Directions

Use a 6-quart slow cooker. Place the chicken into the bottom of your cooker. Add the vegetables and garlic. Pour in the can of tomatoes and stir in the seasonings. Cover and cook on low for 6 to 8 hours. Shred the chicken with forks and serve over hot pasta (I used brown rice fusilli).

The Verdict

This classic comfort dish couldn't be any easier or taste any better. Slow cooking allows all the flavors to intermingle and create a fantastic flavor.

CHICKEN WITH APRICOTS AND DATES

serves 6

The Ingredients

1½ pounds chicken meat (boneless, skinless thighs are the best. If you're going to use chicken with bones, fish them out about halfway through cooking)

1 large yellow onion, finely diced

1 teaspoon ground cumin

½ teaspoon ground cinnamon

½ cup coarsely chopped dried apricots

½ cup coarsely chopped dried pitted dates

¾ cup chicken broth

¼ cup orange juice

cooked quinoa or brown rice for serving

The Directions

Put the chicken into the bottom of a 4- to 6-quart slow cooker. My chicken was frozen solid. If you are using fresh chicken, shave off about 90 minutes or so of cooking time. Add the diced onion and spices. Sprinkle on the apricots and dates. Pour the broth and orange juice evenly over the top. Cover and cook on low for 6 to 7 hours, or on high for 3 to 5 hours. The chicken should be quite tender and shred easily with a fork. If your chicken isn't tender enough, stir well and cook for a bit longer on low.

Serve over quinoa or brown rice with a ladleful of the juices—the broth is delicious!

The Verdict

Don't be turned off by the name of this recipe or the list of ingredients. It sounds a bit odd, I know—dried apricots? dried dates? *with chicken*? Trust me, this tastes good. The chicken gets super tender, with just a touch of sweetness. The dried fruit softens immensely and kind of becomes one with the cooking liquid. The most expensive component to this dish is the dried fruit. My local grocery store sells dried fruit in packages for $2.99, but you can buy it in bulk at a much lower price.

GREEN PEPPER CHICKEN

serves 4

The Ingredients

3 chicken breast halves

2 large green bell peppers, seeded and chopped

1 (7-ounce) can whole or diced green chiles (mine were mild)

1/2 teaspoon dried basil

1 yellow onion, finely diced, or 1 tablespoon dried minced onion

1 teaspoon kosher salt

1/2 teaspoon black pepper

1/4 cup water

1/2 cup sour cream (to add before serving)

corn tortillas or cooked rice (optional)

The Directions

Use a 4-quart slow cooker. Put the chicken in the bottom of the cooker, and add the bell peppers and the chiles. Add the basil, onion, salt, and pepper, and stir a bit to combine. Pour in the water. Cover and cook on low for about 6 hours, or on high for 3 to 4 hours.

Before serving, use tongs to remove the chicken and set aside. Use a handheld stick blender to blend the peppers and sauce left at the bottom of the slow cooker. If you don't have this type of blender, carefully(!) pour the slow cooker contents into a traditional stand blender and pulse until fully combined. Pour back into the slow cooker.

Stir in the sour cream until fully melted. Slice the chicken and return it to the pot. Set to high for 20 to 30 minutes, or until your dinner is hot. Serve the meat in corn tortillas or over rice, if desired.

The Verdict

I've gone on record saying I don't like green peppers. I really don't—they remind me of soggy pizza from my elementary school cafeteria. But they are much less expensive than red, yellow, or orange peppers, and since the flavor is so pronounced, a little goes a long way. I'm happy to report that I really liked the flavor when they are cooked like this, and when paired with the chiles. The chicken turned green, which the kids thought was neat.

HERB GARDEN CHICKEN

serves 4

The Ingredients

1 (5-pound) whole chicken, skinned
$\frac{1}{4}$ cup powdered Parmesan cheese
1 tablespoon dried parsley
1 teaspoon dried sage
1 teaspoon dried rosemary
1 teaspoon dried thyme
1 teaspoon garlic powder
2 tablespoons olive oil

The Directions

Use a 6-quart slow cooker. Using poultry shears, skin the chicken the best you can, and remove the neck and gizzards from the body cavity. In a small mixing bowl, combine the Parmesan cheese and spices. Rub the olive oil all over the bird inside and out. Sprinkle on the cheese and herb mixture, rubbing in and making sure to get a bunch inside. Do not add water. Cover and cook on low for 7 to 8 hours, or on high for 4 to 5 hours. Check the internal temperature of the chicken with a meat thermometer to ensure doneness. The meat will be quite tender and will fall off the bones.

The Verdict

This is a great whole chicken recipe. I usually cook my sides separately, but if you'd like to make a complete one-pot meal, throw in some quartered potatoes and your favorite vegetables. The seasoning blend is magnificent, and Simon and Garfunkel would approve!

HERB-ROASTED CHICKEN
WITH SUMMER TOMATOES

serves 6

The Ingredients

1½ teaspoons kosher salt

1 teaspoon black pepper

2 teaspoons herbes de Provence (sold in the spice aisle, or make your own with the recipe below)

1 teaspoon smoked paprika

4 pounds chicken (whole or parts, your choice)

8 vine-ripened tomatoes

½ cup white wine (you can use apple juice)

HOMEMADE HERBES DE PROVENCE

1 teaspoon dried basil

1 teaspoon dried thyme

1 teaspoon ground rosemary

1 teaspoon dried marjoram

1 teaspoon dried savory

½ teaspoon dried lavender (optional, but traditional)

½ teaspoon dried oregano

½ teaspoon dried sage

The Directions

Use a 6-quart slow cooker. In a small bowl, combine the dry spices and set aside. Wash the chicken, remove the neck and giblets, and try to cut off as much skin as you can using poultry shears. If the

(CONTINUED)

chicken is fully thawed, this is much easier to do. Rub the seasoning mixture on all sides of the bird, inside and out, and place into your stoneware. I chose to put the chicken breast-side down to keep it extra moist.

Wash the tomatoes, cut the stemmy part out of each tomato and discard, and plop the tomatoes on top. Pour in the white wine and cover the slow cooker. Cook on low for about 7 hours, or on high for 4 to 5 hours.

Carefully remove the bird from the pot, and retain the drippings to use in a pot of steamed rice either in a rice cooker or on the stovetop (follow the directions on the rice package).

The Verdict

I loved this meal. The chicken was cooked perfectly (I did 2 hours on high, 3 hours on low, and then it sat on warm for another hour) and the tomatoes were amazing. I am so glad to have made rice with the pan drippings—it was a delicious side.

JAPANESE TAKEOUT TURKEY

serves 4

The Ingredients

3 to 4 pounds turkey drumsticks (2 large)

2 tablespoons gluten-free soy sauce

1 tablespoon brown sugar

1 tablespoon apple cider vinegar

2 garlic cloves, minced

ASIAN SLAW

1 cup shredded red cabbage

1 cup shredded green cabbage

1 cup shredded carrot

2 tablespoons olive oil

1 tablespoon gluten-free soy sauce

1 tablespoon brown sugar

1 tablespoon lemon juice

The Directions

Use a 4-quart slow cooker. Place 2 turkey drumsticks in the bottom of your slow cooker. I always try to remove as much skin as I can when using poultry—but it's your choice. In a small bowl, combine the soy sauce, brown sugar, vinegar, and minced garlic. Pour the sauce over the turkey legs, then flip the drumsticks over a few times so they are evenly coated on each side. Cover and cook on low for 6 to 7 hours, or on high for about 4 hours. Serve on top of Asian Slaw.

Make the slaw: While the turkey is cooking, prepare the slaw in a large mixing bowl. Combine the shredded cabbage with the carrot and set aside. Prepare the dressing in a small bowl by whisking together the olive oil, soy sauce, brown sugar, and lemon juice. Toss the cabbage and carrot with the dressing, and refrigerate until serving time.

(CONTINUED)

The Verdict

Turkey legs cook wonderfully in the slow cooker—they become tender and the meat falls away from the bone nicely. I need to remember to make turkey more often than just during the holidays! The crunchy slaw was a great side dish—and a fantastic way to get more veggies into the kids.

NOT-SO-SLOPPY JOES

serves 8

The Ingredients

2 pounds extra-lean ground turkey
1/2 cup brown sugar
2 cups ketchup
1/2 cup Dijon mustard
1/4 cup A-1 steak sauce
rolls or rice cakes for serving

The Directions

Use a 6-quart slow cooker. Put the ground meat directly into the slow cooker, and add the brown sugar, ketchup, mustard, and A-1. Stir well with a spoon to combine the flavors. (If you don't have extra-lean turkey in the house or you choose to use a different variety of meat, you may want to brown the meat on the stove and drain the fat before putting it into the slow cooker with the rest of the ingredients.)

Cover and cook on low for 8 hours, or on high for 4 hours. Stir well to break up the meat before serving on rolls or rice cakes.

The Verdict

I'm a bit surprised at how much I liked these! The meat is sweet with a bit of a tang from the Dijon and A-1 sauce. These were super easy to throw together, and quite filling. Since the meat doesn't need to be browned before placing into the slow cooker, this is a great candidate for a "TV Dinner" meal (described on page 6).

PESTO CHICKEN AND SWEET POTATOES LAYERED DINNER

serves 4

The Ingredients

PESTO

¼ cup olive oil

2 tablespoons lemon or lime juice

4 garlic cloves

2 cups fresh basil leaves

2 tablespoons pine nuts, walnuts, or sunflower seeds

¼ teaspoon pepper

¼ teaspoon salt

4 chicken thighs or breast halves

sliced mozzarella cheese (I've used string cheese!)

aluminum foil or parchment paper

4 small sweet potatoes, washed well, skin on

The Directions

Use a 6-quart slow cooker. In a food processor or blender, combine the ingredients for your pesto. When liquidy, taste. If you need to add more citrus or salt or pepper, do so now.

In the bottom of a large slow cooker, arrange your chicken pieces. Layer on slices of mozzarella cheese. Pour the pesto evenly on top. Cover with a layer of foil or parchment paper. Scrub the sweet potatoes well, prick with a fork, and lay them on top of the paper or foil. Cover and cook on low for 6 to 7 hours, or on high for 4 to 5 hours.

If you're using fresh chicken and your sweet potatoes are quite large, you may choose to swap layers and put the sweet potatoes on the bottom. Newer slow cookers cook from the sides as well as from the bottom, but some people swear that the stuff on the bottom cooks faster.

Carefully remove the sweet potatoes with tongs, and remove the foil or parchment. The steam that comes out will be quite hot—keep small children away.

The Verdict

We all loved this meal. My kids put cinnamon on their sweet potatoes and enjoyed eating the skin. The chicken was fully cooked, and the pesto had a good bite from the garlic that was balanced by the citrus. I used limes instead of lemons, and enjoyed the lime-y flavor. Lots of pesto calls for gobs of Parmesan cheese, which I opted not to use to 1) keep it a bit lighter and 2) save a trip to the store.

PIZZA CHICKEN

serves 4

The Ingredients

4 chicken breast halves
1 green bell pepper, seeded and sliced
1 small yellow onion, peeled and diced
1 (14-ounce) jar pizza sauce
4 cups shredded mozzarella cheese

The Directions

Use a 4-quart slow cooker. Place the chicken in the bottom of your removable stoneware insert. Dump the vegetables on top. Pour in the pizza sauce and add the cheese. Cover and cook on low for 6 to 7 hours, or on high for 4 hours.

The Verdict

My kids loved this chicken and ate a lot of it, as did our three-year-old friend Max. This is kid-pleasing food! I usually prefer to cook with thighs for the added punch of flavor and juice, but I found that the cheese and sauce give off plenty of flavor to season the breasts perfectly.

BEEF & PORK

Big Easy Meatloaf   *178*

Chili Macaroni and Cheese   *180*

Dry Rub Ribs   *181*

Greek Ribs   *182*

Pear and Ginger Pork Chops   *184*

Peperoncini Beef Sandwiches   *185*

Root Beer Pulled Pork   *186*

Simple Pepper Steak   *187*

Super Simple Cranberry Roast   *188*

Sweet and Savory Pot Roast   *189*

Sweet Mustard Roast   *190*

Taco Pie   *191*

BIG EASY MEATLOAF

serves 6

The Ingredients

1 pound lean ground turkey or beef
1 small onion, chopped
2 fully cooked andouille sausage links (6 ounces total), casing removed and finely chopped
1 teaspoon garlic powder
1/4 teaspoon paprika
1/4 teaspoon dried thyme
1/4 teaspoon ground cumin
1/2 teaspoon kosher salt
1/4 teaspoon pepper
1 egg, lightly beaten
cooking spray

The Directions

Use a 6-quart slow cooker, with an inserted 9 x 5 x 3-inch metal or glass loaf pan. In a mixing bowl, combine all the ingredients with your hands until fully mixed. Spray the inside of your loaf pan well with cooking spray. Press the meat mixture into the loaf pan and lower it inside the slow cooker stoneware. Do not add water. Cover and cook on low for 6 to 8 hours, or on high for 3 to 5 hours. Your meatloaf will brown on top and pull slightly away from the sides when fully cooked. Check doneness with an inserted knife or meat thermometer. Let sit with the slow cooker lid off and the machine unplugged for 15 minutes before removing the pan (carefully—use oven gloves!) from the pot.

The Verdict

This is a fun twist on traditional meatloaf. The andouille sausage does a great job of jazzing up ground turkey meat, which can sometimes be quite boring on its own. Serve sliced with steamed vegetables and potato wedges (try the Irish Potatoes on page 58). My kids like to dip their meatloaf in ketchup and A-1® sauce.

CHILI MACARONI AND CHEESE

serves 6

The Ingredients

1 pound lean ground beef, browned and drained
1 onion, finely diced
1 (14.5-ounce) can diced tomatoes, undrained
1 (15-ounce) can kidney beans, undrained
2 teaspoons chili powder
1 teaspoon ground cumin
2 cups elbow macaroni (I used Trader Joe's brown rice penne)
2 cups Mexican blend shredded cheese

The Directions

Use a 6-quart slow cooker. Brown the meat and onion in a large skillet on the stovetop, and drain the fat. Put into the slow cooker, and add the tomatoes and kidney beans. Stir in the chili powder, cumin, uncooked macaroni, and cheese. Cover and cook on low for 4 hours, or until the pasta has reached the desired tenderness.

The Verdict

This is fantastic. My family adores this cheesy chili pasta and happily gobbles it up. I was really pleased at how the pasta cooked without needing to add any water or additional juice. The moisture of the meat, beans, and tomatoes was plenty. Neat!

DRY RUB RIBS

serves 4

The Ingredients

3 to 4 pounds ribs (beef or pork, your choice)
1 tablespoon dried oregano
1 teaspoon ground cinnamon
1 teaspoon garlic powder
1 teaspoon onion powder
1 teaspoon paprika
1/2 teaspoon crushed red pepper flakes
1/3 cup brown sugar

The Directions

Use a 4-quart slow cooker. Put the ribs directly into the slow cooker. In a bowl, combine all the spices and the brown sugar. Dump the mixture onto the ribs, rubbing around to get the ribs fully coated. Do not add water. Cover and cook on low for 6 to 8 hours, or until the meat is bite-tender. I like my meat to be so tender, it falls completely off the bones.

The Verdict

I love it that you can throw in ribs without any liquid and they will steam and cook to perfection in the slow cooker. This spice rub is fantastic—it's sure to please everyone. The cinnamon provides a fantastic smoky flavor, and is a happy surprise for your taste buds. I served our ribs with mashed potatoes, and Cauliflower Gratin (page 148).

GREEK RIBS

serves 4

The Ingredients

4 pounds pork spareribs
1/4 cup brown sugar
1 tablespoon kosher salt
1 tablespoon garlic powder
1 teaspoon ground coriander
1/2 teaspoon fennel seeds
1 teaspoon ground cumin
1 teaspoon ground anise
1 teaspoon dry mustard
1 teaspoon ground cinnamon
1 tablespoon honey
1/2 cup orange juice
1/2 teaspoon whole black peppercorns
4 whole cloves

The Directions

Use a 4-quart slow cooker. Put the ribs into the bottom of a slow cooker. In a small bowl, mix together the brown sugar and spices. Rub the mixture on all sides of the ribs. Add the honey, orange juice, whole peppercorns, and cloves. Cover and cook on low for 8 hours, or on high for 4 to 5. Your ribs are done when they have reached the desired tenderness. I like them to be so tender the meat falls off the bone.

The Verdict

I LOVE THESE RIBS!

There is a long laundry list of spices included in this spice rub, but hopefully most of the spices are already residing somewhere in your kitchen cabinets. This spice combo would make an old leather shoe taste good.

PEAR AND GINGER PORK CHOPS

serves 4

The Ingredients

4 pork chops
1 (15-ounce) can sliced pears
1 teaspoon ground ginger
2 tablespoons apple cider vinegar

The Directions

Use a 4-quart slow cooker. Put the chops into the slow cooker, and pour in the entire can of pears. Add the ginger and vinegar. Cover and cook on low for 6 to 8 hours, or until the chops are thoroughly cooked and have reached the desired tenderness.

The Verdict

This is the easiest recipe, yet it tastes fantastic. The spice from the ginger works well with the sweetness from the pears. This makes a fantastic summertime meal. Many people forget about their slow cooker in the summer months, but I really like using it on a hot day because the kitchen doesn't heat up the way it would if I turned on the stove or oven. Serve your chop with a nice leafy salad out in the yard!

PEPERONCINI BEEF SANDWICHES

serves 6

The Ingredients

2 pounds beef chuck roast

1 (16-ounce) jar peperoncini peppers

6 ounces sliced mozzarella or Swiss cheese

6 hamburger buns or French rolls (I used gluten-free toasted bread)

The Directions

Use a 4-quart slow cooker. Put the chuck roast into the cooker. Pour in the entire jar of peperoncini peppers. Cover and cook on low for 8 to 10 hours, or until the meat shreds easily with a fork. Shred the meat completely, and serve with sliced cheese on toasted buns or rolls.

The Verdict

What a great sandwich! If you're gluten-free and don't have bread in the house, you can serve the meat over a plate of rice or on a lightly salted rice cake. It's delicious. The meat gives off a great deal of juice while it's cooking, which mellows the sometimes harsh taste of the peperoncinis tremendously.

ROOT BEER PULLED PORK

serves 6

The Ingredients

2 pounds boneless pork shoulder roast

1 large onion, sliced in rings

1 to 2 tablespoons Tabasco sauce (start with 1—you can increase to taste after cooking)

1 cup chili sauce (near the ketchup in the grocery store)

2 cups root beer

$1/2$ teaspoon vanilla extract

6 hamburger buns or soft rolls (I make rolls out of a gluten-free bread mix)

The Directions

Use a 4-quart slow cooker. Put the meat into the slow cooker and add the onion slices. Top with the Tabasco sauce, chili sauce, root beer, and vanilla. Cover and cook on low for 8 to 10 hours, or until the pork shreds easily with a fork. Shred completely, and serve on toasted buns or rolls.

The Verdict

The root beer flavor is evident! I received this recipe from Monique, who calls this her "one successful slow cooker recipe." She's right—not only is this successful, it's absolutely delicious. We shared the leftover meat with friends, and they too commented on how much flavor the root beer provides. What fun!

SIMPLE PEPPER STEAK

serves 4

The Ingredients

1 pound beef round, cut in strips

1 (14.5-ounce) can Italian stewed tomatoes

3 tablespoons tomato paste

1 teaspoon gluten-free Worcestershire sauce

1/4 teaspoon kosher salt

1/4 teaspoon pepper

1 (16-ounce) bag frozen stir-fry peppers (thawed, to add at the end of cooking time)

cooked brown rice or quinoa for serving

The Directions

Use a 4-quart slow cooker. Put the meat into the bottom of your slow cooker. Add the tomatoes, tomato paste, Worcestershire sauce, salt, and pepper. Stir with a wooden spoon to combine. Cover and cook on low for 6 hours, or on high for 3 to 4 hours. Add the peppers and stir well. Cover again and cook on high for 20 to 30 minutes, or until the peppers are heated through. Serve over a big plate of brown rice or quinoa.

The Verdict

We ate this for dinner between rushing around for softball practice and a PTA meeting. It was nice to sit down and have a great meal with very little work. I set up the rice cooker to cook quinoa and stirred in the peppers while the kids cleaned up and changed out of their softball clothes.

SUPER SIMPLE CRANBERRY ROAST

serves 4

The Ingredients

2 to 3 pounds beef or pork roast or stew chunks

1 tablespoon dried onion flakes or 1 medium yellow onion, diced

2 tablespoons gluten-free soy sauce

1 (16-ounce) can whole berry cranberry sauce

The Directions

Use a 4-quart slow cooker. Plop in the meat (frozen is fine), and add the onion and soy sauce. Pour the cranberry sauce over the top. Do not add water. Cover and cook on low for 7 to 9 hours, or on high for 5 to 6 hours. If you are cooking on high, you may need to "help" the meat break apart by taking it out an hour or so before serving by cutting it into chunks, then returning it to the sauce. I like it when the meat is tender and the juice has fully soaked in.

Serve over mashed potatoes with a green salad.

The Verdict

This was a fantastic dinner, and since everything was already in the house, it was free!

The meat was sweet (but not overly so), tender, and moist, and everyone at the table had seconds.

I used frozen beef chuck, but this would be fantastic with any hunk of meat you've got lying around—beef, pork, or venison.

SWEET AND SAVORY POT ROAST

serves 6

The Ingredients

    4 pounds beef rump or chuck roast
    2 onions, sliced in rings
    1/4 cup brown sugar
    1/2 cup apple cider vinegar
    1 cup ketchup
    2 cups baby carrots
    2 cups beef broth
    garlic mashed potatoes for serving

The Directions

Use a 6-quart slow cooker. Put the roast into the slow cooker. Add the onion slices, separated into rings. Pour in the brown sugar, vinegar, and ketchup. Toss in the carrots. Pour the beef broth evenly over the top. Cover and cook on low for 6 to 8 hours, or until the meat has reached the desired tenderness. If you'd like your meat even more tender, take it out 1 hour before dinnertime and cut it into thirds. Return the meat to the pot and turn to high. Serve over garlic mashed potatoes with a ladleful of juice.

The Verdict

I love this roast. Sometimes pot roast can become boring. Surprise your family with this recipe—it's definitely not dull, and since it utilizes pantry staples, it's a great choice to insert into a busy week's meal plan.

SWEET MUSTARD ROAST

serves 4

The Ingredients

3 pounds beef or pork roast (mine was still frozen when I put it in)
⅓ cup molasses
⅓ cup Dijon mustard
2 tablespoons white vinegar (apple cider vinegar would work well, too)
1 teaspoon garlic powder

The Directions

Use a 4-quart slow cooker. Dump meat into the cooker. Top with the molasses, mustard, and vinegar. Toss in the garlic powder. Using tongs, flip the meat over a few times to coat it nicely with the sauce. Cover and cook on low for 6 to 8 hours, or on high for about 4. If your meat isn't as tender as you'd like after cooking time has elapsed, take it out and cut it into a few pieces, then return it to the pot. Roasts are best when cooked on low for a long period of time.

The Verdict

I served this meat the night we got our Christmas tree. I have a video of the kids eating the meat and making yummy noises while we were trying to untangle the lights. It was a fun night, and the meal was successful. I served mashed potatoes and green beans for sides, and they were a nice complement.

TACO PIE

serves 6

The Ingredients

1 pound lean ground beef, browned and drained

1 large onion, diced

½ cup salsa

1 (1.25-ounce) packet taco seasoning (the McCormick brand is gluten-free, or see page 27 to make your own)

1 cup shredded cheddar cheese

½ cup biscuit/baking mix (I use a gluten-free baking mix)

2 eggs

1 cup milk

6 tablespoons sour cream (optional)

corn tortilla chips (optional)

The Directions

Use a 4-quart slow cooker. Put the ground beef into your slow cooker stoneware insert. Add the diced onion and salsa. Stir in the contents of the taco seasoning packet. Top the mixture with the shredded cheese. In a small mixing bowl, combine the baking/biscuit mix with the eggs and milk, and whisk together until a batter forms. Pour evenly over the top of the cheese. Cover and cook on low for 6 hours, or on high for 3 to 4 hours. Remove the lid of the slow cooker and continue cooking on high for 20 to 30 minutes to cook away condensation. You will know your topping is done when it is browned, an inserted knife comes out clean, and it has pulled away from the sides. Serve with a dollop of sour cream and a handful of tortilla chips, if desired.

(CONTINUED)

The Verdict

The kids, Adam, and I all love this meal. It's a great way to get a taco fix at the end of a busy day. I like to keep already browned and drained meat in one-pound measurements in plastic zippered bags in the freezer. I thaw it the night before in the refrigerator, which saves valuable time in the morning.

DESSERTS

Apple Coffee Cake   *194*

Chocolate Pot de Crème with Ganache   *196*

Holiday Pears   *197*

Raspberry Fondue   *198*

Sugared Cinnamon Almonds   *199*

APPLE COFFEE CAKE

serves 8

The Ingredients

COFFEE CAKE

cooking spray

2 cups Bisquick® mix (I used a gluten-free baking mix)

²/₃ cup applesauce

¼ cup milk

2 tablespoons sugar

2 tablespoons butter, melted

2 green apples, peeled, cored, and diced

1 teaspoon ground cinnamon

1 teaspoon vanilla extract

1 egg

CRUMB TOPPING

¼ cup Bisquick® (I used a gluten-free baking mix)

¼ cup brown sugar

2 tablespoons butter, softened

¼ cup chopped nuts (optional)

The Directions

Use a 4-quart slow cooker sprayed with cooking spray. In a large mixing bowl, combine all the ingredients for the coffee cake. Stir with a rubber spatula to combine. The batter will be thick and lumpy. Pour into the prepared stoneware insert. In a small bowl, combine the ingredients for the crumb topping. Sprinkle the topping evenly over the cake batter. Cover and cook on high for 2 to 3 hours, or until the cake browns on top and pulls away from the sides. Uncover and cook on high for another 30 minutes, or until a toothpick inserted in the middle comes out clean.

The Verdict

Yummy! This is a great coffee cake. It also freezes really well—which I like to do in small containers to thaw and heat in the microwave on busy mornings.

CHOCOLATE POT DE CRÈME WITH GANACHE

serves 8

The Ingredients

5 egg yolks
2 cups heavy cream
$\frac{1}{2}$ cup baker's sugar (because the granules are fine)
1 tablespoon vanilla extract
$\frac{1}{4}$ cup unsweetened cocoa powder

GANACHE TOPPING

$\frac{1}{2}$ cup chocolate chips
$\frac{1}{2}$ cup heavy cream

The Directions

Use a 6-quart slow cooker with an inserted oven-safe dish (Pyrex® or Corningware®) that fits all the way inside your stoneware. I use a 1 $\frac{1}{2}$-quart casserole dish. Add water around the dish until reaching the halfway point (you're using the slow cooker as a bain-marie, or water bath.)

In a mixing bowl, whip together the egg yolks, cream, sugar, vanilla, and cocoa powder. Pour the mixture into the dish, and cook on high for 2 to 4 hours. Your custard should be set in the center (check by lightly touching with your finger) with the middle still a bit jiggly. Unplug the slow cooker, and let it cool down enough to safely remove the inserted dish. Cool in the refrigerator for 2 to 3 hours before topping with the ganache.

Make the ganache: Melt the chocolate chips in the microwave, whisk in the cream until fully incorporated, and pour evenly over the top. Return to the refrigerator for another 2 to 3 hours before serving.

The Verdict

Heavenly chocolate goodness. The chocolate mousse part was rich and creamy—the kind of richness that makes your eyes go a tiny bit crossed. The four of us who could eat this wonderful dessert (the baby was only a few weeks old) dipped our spoons right into the baking dish.

HOLIDAY PEARS

serves 8

The Ingredients

8 firm ripe pears (I like red d'Anjou)
1/2 cup dried unsweetened cranberries
1 cup sugar
1/4 teaspoon ground ginger
1/4 teaspoon ground cinnamon
1/8 teaspoon ground cloves
1 lemon, juiced
2 tablespoons apple cider vinegar

The Directions

Use a 6-quart slow cooker. Peel the pears but leave them whole (they are slippery when peeled, so be careful!). Stand the pears upright in your slow cooker (I was able to get all 8 into my oval 6-quart comfortably). Sprinkle on the cranberries. In a small bowl, combine the sugar, ginger, cinnamon, and cloves, and spoon on top of the pears. Pour the lemon juice and apple cider vinegar evenly over the contents. Cover and cook on low for 4 hours, or on high for about 2 hours.

The Verdict

This is a fantastic dessert to share with company—the pears present fabulously. Serve in a shallow bowl, standing, with a spoonful of the accumulated juice and cranberries.

RASPBERRY FONDUE

serves 8 to 10

The Ingredients

1 cup heavy whipping cream
1 (12-ounce) bag white chocolate chips
1 cup seedless raspberry jam
cookies, apple slices, or marshmallows for dipping

The Directions

Use a 2-quart slow cooker. Put the cream, chocolate chips, and jam into your slow cooker. Heat on low for 1 hour, then stir well. Cover again and heat for another 2 hours, or until the fondue is hot and bubbly. Use cookies (I like gluten-free gingersnaps or animal cookies), apple slices, or marsh-mallows as dippers.

The Verdict

Denise M. sent me this recipe—she saw it originally written in a Tupperware® catalog (I love Tupperware® parties) and thought it would work well in a tiny slow cooker. She's right! The white chocolate and raspberry combination is a winner, and my kids and their friends loved it. I liked using Granny Smith apple slices the best for dipping.

SUGARED CINNAMON ALMONDS

serves 10

The Ingredients

cooking spray
$1^1/_2$ cups sugar
3 tablespoons ground cinnamon
$1/_8$ teaspoon kosher salt
1 egg white
$1^1/_2$ teaspoons vanilla extract
$3^1/_4$ cups whole raw almonds
aluminum foil or parchment paper

The Directions

Use a 4-quart slow cooker. Spray your stoneware insert well with cooking spray. In a mixing bowl, combine the sugar, cinnamon, and salt; set aside. In a large mixing bowl, whisk together the egg white and vanilla, pour in the almonds, and toss to coat. Add the cinnamon mixture, and toss the nuts well to coat evenly. Pour into your slow cooker. Cover and cook on high for 2 hours, stirring every 20 to 30 minutes. When the nuts are hot and toasty, pour out on a length of aluminum foil or parchment paper and let sit until cool. Store in an airtight container.

The Verdict

These didn't last very long in our house. The almonds get coated nicely and remind me of the little cellophane bags of nuts sold at the farmers' market. Delicious. These nuts make a fantastic home-made gift.

$15
and
Under

*W*hat can you get for $15? An awful lot! The recipes in this section of the book were all prepared for under $15, and most of them cost around $11 or $12—just a touch above the ones in the previous section. I LOVE that I can entertain a houseful of people with an impressive main course such as Beef Bourguignon (page 258), or our new favorite to serve at parties, Country Captain (page 245), for less than it would cost to buy only one plateful at a restaurant.

There are also some amazing soups and stews listed in this section that are actually very hearty main courses. Three of our absolute favorites are the Big Bayou Jambalaya (page 219), Mulligatawny (page 222), and New England Clam Chowder (page 223).

You'll notice that there are many more beef and pork main-course dishes and there aren't any vegetarian options. That's because larger cuts of meat naturally cost more, and it's difficult to pay a lot for a vegetarian meal! Many of the soups, stews, and bean dishes in this section can be made without a drop of meat, though, and one of the best-reviewed chilis on my Web site is the vegan Sweet Potato Chili on page 231.

Many of the recipes listed here make more than the traditional four servings, and are fantastic for large families or for entertaining. Or you can freeze the leftovers to enjoy again on a terribly busy night.

As in the other sections, I have rounded up in my price estimates—you can certainly use coupons to save even more money, or make your own broth instead of using store-bought the way I did.

BEVERAGES

Boston Tea Punch   *204*

Caribbean Coffee   *205*

BOSTON TEA PUNCH

serves 4

The Ingredients
2 cups water
2 black tea bags
1/2 cup rum
2 ounces Triple Sec
2 tablespoons sugar
8 lemon slices

The Directions
Use a 2-quart slow cooker. Put the water into the slow cooker and add the tea bags. Pour in the rum and Triple Sec, and stir in the sugar. Float the lemon slices on top. Cover and cook on low for 4 hours, or on high for about 2 hours. Squeeze out the tea bags and discard before serving.

The Verdict
Thank you to Barbara for this recipe! She serves it for her book club (and now I'm thinking my book club is rather boring). This is some Very. Powerful. Punch. I shared it with some friends, who really liked it a lot.

CARIBBEAN COFFEE

serves 4

The Ingredients

3 cups strong black coffee

$2/3$ cup dark rum

2 tablespoons sugar

2 teaspoons coconut extract

whipped cream as garnish (optional)

The Directions

Use a 2-quart slow cooker. Stir the coffee, rum, sugar, and extract together in the cooker. Cover and cook on low for 4 hours, or on high for about 2 hours. Ladle into mugs and top with whipped cream, if desired. This is an excellent after-dinner drink.

The Verdict

You will feel cozy drinking this coffee. You can tell the rum is in there, but it balances nicely with the coffee and coconut. This would be lovely to drink outdoors around a campfire, or indoors huddled around a wood-burning stove on a stormy night. Or you can just plug in your slow cooker on the kitchen countertop on a boring Wednesday evening to liven up your week.

BREAKFASTS

Cheesy Sausage Breakfast Bake   *207*

Maple Banana Oat Bread   *208*

Sausage and Tomato Breakfast Casserole   *210*

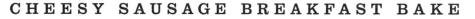

CHEESY SAUSAGE BREAKFAST BAKE

serves 8

The Ingredients

1 (30-ounce) package frozen hash brown potatoes
1 pound breakfast sausage, crumbled
1 onion, diced
1 (16-ounce) container light cottage cheese
3 eggs, lightly beaten
4 slices American cheese, cut in pieces
1/2 teaspoon kosher salt
1/4 teaspoon black pepper

The Directions

Use a 6-quart slow cooker. Dump the frozen hash browns into the bottom of your stoneware insert. In a large mixing bowl, combine the crumbled sausage, onion, cottage cheese, eggs, American cheese, salt, and pepper. Mix well and pour over the potatoes. Cover and cook on low for 6 to 8 hours. I set my slow cooker to cook for 7 hours overnight, then let it stay on warm until breakfast time. You will know your casserole is finished when it has browned on top and begun to pull away from the sides.

The Verdict

We all really love this breakfast bake, and have served it twice to overnight company with rave reviews. It's so tasty, I usually enjoy the leftovers cold. This freezes and reheats quite well, too. I like that I can throw this together when we're running low on eggs.

MAPLE BANANA OAT BREAD

serves 4

The Ingredients

1½ cups all-purpose flour (I use a gluten-free baking mix)

1 teaspoon baking powder

½ teaspoon ground cinnamon

¾ cup rolled oats

½ cup brown sugar

1 teaspoon vanilla extract

1½ cups smashed bananas (3 large)

2 tablespoons maple syrup

¼ cup butter, melted

1 large egg

The Directions

Use a 6-quart slow cooker with an inserted 9 × 5 × 3-inch loaf pan. In a large mixing bowl, combine all the dry ingredients. Whisk in the vanilla, bananas, maple syrup, butter, and egg. When fully combined, pour the batter into a greased loaf pan. Place the loaf pan into your slow cooker insert. Do not add water. Cover, but prop the lid open with the end of a wooden spoon or skewer. Cook on high for 4 hours, or until your banana bread is brown on top, has pulled away from the sides, and an inserted toothpick comes out clean. Unplug the cooker and let the pan cool for 20 to 30 minutes before removing from the crock—it'll be hot, so be careful and use oven gloves!

The Verdict

People sometimes ask why I like to bake in the slow cooker since it takes so much longer than it does to just plop the bread or cake into the oven. It does definitely take longer, but I like that I can whisk together the batter, put it into the slow cooker, and leave the house to run errands or pick up the kids from school. I also really appreciate that if I'm running a few minutes late, the slow cooker will turn to a warm setting and wait for me to arrive home to check the progress.

SAUSAGE AND TOMATO BREAKFAST CASSEROLE

serves 8 to 10

The Ingredients

2 pounds mixed-color cherry tomatoes

2 pounds smoked Italian sausage, sliced (I used 1 pound sweet, 1 pound spicy)

2 small yellow onions, sliced

3 bell peppers (red, yellow, orange)

3 medium-sized russet potatoes, diced

1 tablespoon Italian seasoning

1/2 teaspoon kosher salt

The Directions

Use a 6-quart slow cooker. Wash the cherry tomatoes and toss into your slow cooker. Add the sausage, onions, bell peppers, and potatoes. Sprinkle in the Italian seasoning and salt, and stir to combine. Do not add water. Cover and cook on low for 6 to 8 hours. If the tomatoes don't pop right away, turn to high for about an hour, or until the tomatoes are mostly squished. I set my slow cooker to cook on low for 7 hours overnight, and it stays warm until breakfast time.

The Verdict

We had this on Easter morning for breakfast, and it was wonderful. Twelve of us enjoyed this dish (it was a potluck—there was a lot of food on the table!) and happily gobbled it up. This is a great breakfast option for those who don't like (or choose not to eat) eggs. Thank you so much to Ruby for sending me her recipe!

APPETIZERS

Apricot Barbecue Wings   *212*

Beer and Cheddar Fondue   *213*

Meatballs in Peanut Chili Sauce   *214*

Pineapple Party Meatballs   *215*

APRICOT BARBECUE WINGS

serves 8

The Ingredients

3 pounds chicken wings (I leave on the wing joints, but you can discard them if you like)
1 cup prepared barbecue sauce
1 (18-ounce) jar apricot preserves
1 teaspoon dry mustard
1 tablespoon Tabasco sauce

The Directions

Use a 6-quart slow cooker. Spread the wings out on a large cookie sheet and bake in the oven at 400°F for 10 minutes, or until browned. Put the wings into the slow cooker. In a bowl, combine the barbecue sauce, apricot preserves, mustard, and Tabasco. Stir well and pour on top of the wings. Cover and cook on low for 5 hours, or until the chicken is cooked through but still attached to the bone.

The Verdict

These wings are lovely—sweet with a pleasant kick at the end. They're sticky, too. Keep wipes close by when feeding children—the stickiness seems to spread.

I usually don't bother to brown meat in the oven before tossing it into the slow cooker, but taking the time to brown these wings cooks the skin a bit so they don't get too soggy in the crock. This bit of browning is primarily for texture—it's not to cook the wings.

BEER AND CHEDDAR FONDUE
serves 8

The Ingredients

½ small yellow onion, peeled and finely minced
1 garlic clove, minced
8 ounces extra sharp cheddar cheese, grated (2 cups)
4 ounces Gruyère cheese, grated (1 cup)
1 tablespoon cornstarch
1 teaspoon dry mustard
1 teaspoon caraway seeds
1 (12-ounce) bottle beer (Redbridge® by Anheuser-Busch is gluten-free)
¼ teaspoon kosher salt
¼ teaspoon freshly ground black pepper
stuff for dipping: crostini (page 24), steamed cauliflower or carrots, apple slices, pickles, or grilled sausage slices

The Directions

Use a 2-quart slow cooker. Put the onion, garlic, and cheeses into your slow cooker. Stir in the cornstarch and dry mustard. Crush the caraway seeds using a mortar and pestle (I don't have one of these, so instead I used a zippered freezer bag and a small mallet), and add to the pot. Pour in the beer. Cover and cook on low for 2 to 4 hours, stirring every 30 minutes. Add the salt and pepper before serving. Leave the slow cooker plugged in and turned to low while serving with the desired dippers.

The Verdict

Fondue is a great snack or appetizer to enjoy with friends, and this dip is a nice alternative to simply melting a block of Velveeta® (not that there's anything wrong with that!). Our friends Jennifer and Adam were over when we made this and we all truly enjoyed it.

MEATBALLS IN PEANUT CHILI SAUCE

serves 10

The Ingredients

40 cooked meatballs, frozen or fresh (Coleman Natural® and Aidells® have a gluten-free variety)

2 tablespoons chunky peanut butter

1 cup canned coconut milk (I used light and it was fine. If using regular, shake well and include the cream on top)

1 tablespoon red chili paste (jarred, in the Asian cooking aisle)

2 teaspoons fish sauce (in the Asian cooking aisle—surprisingly inexpensive, although I bet you could substitute a gluten-free soy sauce and not notice much of a taste difference)

1½ tablespoons sugar

The Directions

Use a 4-quart slow cooker. Put the meatballs into the slow cooker (frozen is fine). Add the peanut butter and coconut milk. Drop in the red chili paste, then add the fish sauce and sugar. Stir as well as you can to combine—it won't be perfect because the peanut butter will still be clumpy. No worries.

Cook on low for 4 to 6 hours, high for 2 to 4, or until the peanut butter mixture is fully melted and the meatballs are heated throughout.

Serve as a hot appetizer or over long-grain basmati rice as a meal.

The Verdict

I made these meatballs for friends, and the seven of us (four adults and three kids, aged three to eight and a half years) all really liked the flavor: creamy and slightly coconutty, with a bit of spice. If your meatballs have a kick to them on their own, cut back on the chili paste. We all really liked the bit of crunch from the chunky peanut butter, but if you aren't a crunchy person, by all means use creamy. I ate three of them cold the next day for breakfast, and they were still quite tasty.

PINEAPPLE PARTY MEATBALLS

serves 10

The Ingredients

40 Italian-style frozen meatballs (Coleman Natural® and Aidells® have a gluten-free variety)
1 (8-ounce) can crushed pineapple, drained
$1/4$ cup ketchup
$1/4$ cup apple cider vinegar
$1/4$ cup brown sugar
$1/4$ cup water

The Directions

Use a 4-quart slow cooker. Put the frozen meatballs into the bottom of your slow cooker. In a mixing bowl, combine the drained pineapple, ketchup, vinegar, brown sugar, and water, and pour over the meatballs.

Cover and cook on low for 4 to 6 hours, on high for 2 hours, or until the meatballs are fully hot. Serve with toothpicks for dipping.

The Verdict

The pineapple sauce creates a sweet glaze for the Italian-style meatballs. I like how these taste different and are "fancier" than using plain ol' barbecue sauce. It's so much fun to eat food off of toothpicks.

SOUPS & STEWS

African Peanut Stew   217

Beer Cheese Soup   218

Big Bayou Jambalaya   219

Crab and Corn Soup   221

Mulligatawny   222

New England Clam Chowder   223

Pesto Minestrone Soup   225

Sweet Potato and Chorizo Soup   226

AFRICAN PEANUT STEW

serves 6

The Ingredients

2 pounds boneless, skinless chicken, cut in 1-inch chunks (I like thighs)

3 sweet potatoes, peeled and chopped in 1-inch chunks

¾ cup all-natural creamy peanut butter

1 (28-ounce) can diced tomatoes, undrained

1½ cups chicken broth

1 tablespoon dried minced onion flakes

1 teaspoon ground ginger

2 tablespoons tomato paste

2 teaspoons curry powder

1 teaspoon red pepper flakes

½ teaspoon kosher salt

2 limes, cut in wedges (for garnish, to add later)

The Directions

Use a 6-quart slow cooker. Put the chicken into the bottom of your slow cooker. Add the sweet potatoes. Plop in the peanut butter, tomatoes, and broth. Add the dried onion and all the spices. Don't worry about stirring now—the peanut butter will make it difficult. Cover and cook on low for 6 to 8 hours, or on high for 4 to 5. Stir well and serve with a squeeze of lime juice in each serving.

The Verdict

This is an amazing stew. It's thick, rich, and hearty and the peanut butter provides a fantastic silky feel on your tongue. We all licked our bowls clean. The leftovers are just as fantastic, and this freezes quite well, but you'll need to thin it with a bit more broth when reheating.

BEER CHEESE SOUP

serves 6

The Ingredients

4 cups chicken broth

1 (12-ounce) bottle beer (Redbridge® by Anheuser-Busch is gluten-free)

16 ounces American cheese, cubed

1 tablespoon gluten-free Worcestershire sauce

2 green onions, diced

1 teaspoon Italian seasoning

1 cup half-and-half (to add later)

6 ounces blue cheese crumbles (to add later)

The Directions

Use a 4-quart slow cooker. Combine the chicken broth and beer in your slow cooker. Add the cheese, Worcestershire sauce, green onions, and Italian seasoning. Cover and cook on low for 4 to 6 hours, or until the cheese has fully melted. Stir well, and slowly add the half-and-half. Serve in small soup or bread bowls, and garnish with a handful of crumbled blue cheese.

The Verdict

Don't try to make an entire meal out of this—it's blissfully rich. I enjoyed my soup as a late lunch with a tuna sandwich and spinach salad. Thank you so much to Emily for sending me this recipe. She used to serve the soup to restaurant patrons, and I can see why!

BIG BAYOU JAMBALAYA

serves 10

The Ingredients

1 pound boneless, skinless chicken, cut in 1-inch chunks

$1/2$ pound smoked kielbasa or Polish sausage, sliced

2 green bell peppers, seeded and diced

2 yellow onions, peeled and chopped

6 garlic cloves, minced

1 (28-ounce) can crushed tomatoes

1 quart chicken broth

$1^1/2$ cups water

$1/2$ cup Dijon mustard

2 tablespoons gluten-free Worcestershire sauce

1 teaspoon cayenne pepper

$1/2$ teaspoon dried thyme

$1/4$ cup chopped fresh flat-leaf parsley

1 pound cooked and peeled frozen shrimp (to add later)

The Directions

Use a 6-quart slow cooker. Although there are a lot of ingredients listed, there really aren't any "rules" to this recipe. Dump everything except the shrimp into your slow cooker, starting with the meat. Cover and cook on low for 8 to 10 hours, or on high for 4 to 6 hours. This soup will taste best when cooked low and slow. Make sure the onions are fully cooked and translucent, then stir in the frozen shrimp 30 minutes before serving. Replace the lid and flip to high. When the shrimp are heated through, ladle into bowls.

(CONTINUED)

The Verdict

I served this jambalaya to friends during the Super Bowl. It's spicy and filling. All the grown-ups in attendance ate healthy servings, but the kids stuck with hot dogs. This recipe makes a lot—it's a wonderful choice for entertaining.

CRAB AND CORN SOUP

serves 6

The Ingredients

1 quart chicken broth

1 tablespoon butter

1 cup chopped onion or 1 tablespoon dried minced onion

1 (32-ounce) package frozen corn

2 garlic cloves, chopped

1 teaspoon kosher salt

$1/2$ teaspoon cayenne pepper

1 (6-ounce) can lump crabmeat, drained

1 cup half-and-half or heavy cream (to add later)

1 avocado, sliced (to add later)

The Directions

Use a 4-quart slow cooker. Pour the broth into the slow cooker, and add the butter and onion. Stir in the frozen corn, garlic, salt, cayenne, and crabmeat. Cover and cook on low for 8 hours, high for 4 hours, or until the onion is cooked through and translucent. If you'd like a thicker broth, pulse a few times with a handheld stick blender, or scoop out a cup of soup and blend in a traditional blender (please be careful—it's very hot!), then stir it back in. Add the half-and-half or cream before serving, and ladle into bowls with avocado slices.

The Verdict

I had this type of soup a few years ago at a restaurant on the wharf in Monterey, and this recipe is quite reminiscent. It's delicious, and I loved the cool contrast of the avocado slices. This is a great soup for lunch, although you could add some cubed potatoes for filler if you'd like to serve it as an evening meal.

MULLIGATAWNY

serves 6

The Ingredients

2 boneless, skinless chicken thighs
1 cup peeled and chopped apple
1 cup chopped carrots
1 (15-ounce) can fire-roasted tomatoes
1 tablespoon dried minced onion flakes
1/4 cup raisins
1 teaspoon lemon juice
2 teaspoons curry powder
1/4 teaspoon ground nutmeg
3 cups chicken broth
1/3 cup long-grain white rice (to add later)

The Directions

Use a 6-quart slow cooker. Put the thighs into the bottom of your cooker. Add the apple, carrots, tomatoes, onion flakes, and raisins. Add the lemon juice, spices, and broth. Cover and cook on low for 8 to 10 hours. Uncover and stir in the uncooked rice. Flip to high for 30 minutes, or until the rice is tender. Shred the chicken thighs with two big forks before ladling into soup bowls.

The Verdict

I have a new favorite meal. I could not get enough of this soup—I had never had anything like it before, and I enjoyed every last drop I could lick out of my bowl. My parents really liked it, too. It's also a lot of fun to say the name! On the famous *Seinfeld* "Soup Nazi" episode, this is the soup Kramer can't get enough of. I can see why!

NEW ENGLAND CLAM CHOWDER

serves 6

The Ingredients

¹/₂ pound sliced bacon, diced

1 (6-ounce) can minced clams, drained

5 small red potatoes, peeled and cut in small chunks

1 onion, minced

1 cup sliced celery

2 garlic cloves, minced

2 teaspoons dried thyme

1 teaspoon dried parsley

1 teaspoon kosher salt

¹/₂ teaspoon pepper

4 cups chicken broth

2 cups half-and-half (to add later)

1 cup shredded cheddar cheese (to add later)

The Directions

Use a 4-quart slow cooker. Brown the bacon on the stovetop and drain the fat. Put the bacon into the bottom of your slow cooker and add the clams. Add the vegetables, spices, and chicken broth. Cover and cook on low for 6 to 8 hours, or until the onion is translucent and the potatoes are tender. Use a handheld stick blender and pulse a few times to blend the potato to thicken the soup. Stir in half-and-half and cheese. Cover and cook on high for 20 to 30 minutes, or until the cheese melts and soup is hot. Serve in bread bowls if you have them! (You can make four bread bowls with a gluten-free bread mix by shaping the mixed dough with your hands and baking them on a parchment-lined cookie sheet according to package directions.)

(CONTINUED)

The Verdict

This is just as wonderful as the soup served on the pier in San Francisco or Monterey. I like thickening soups by blending the ingredients, rather than by making a roux with flour or cornstarch—the bit of mixing with the hand blender brings out the flavor of the vegetables and "awakens" the clams, while naturally thickening the broth to your preferred consistency.

PESTO MINESTRONE SOUP

serves 6

The Ingredients

1 large onion, diced
1 cup chopped carrots
1 cup sliced celery
1 yellow or red bell pepper, seeded and diced
1 pound (any variety) potatoes, cut in 1-inch chunks (no need to peel)
1 (14.5-ounce) can diced tomatoes
2 (15-ounce) cans beans, undrained (your choice, I use 1 black, 1 kidney)
1 (11-ounce) container prepared pesto
4 cups chicken broth
1 cup frozen peas (to add later)
1 handful baby spinach (to add later)

The Directions

Use a 6-quart slow cooker. Put the onion, carrots, celery, pepper, and potatoes into the slow cooker. Add the entire can of tomatoes and the whole cans of beans. Pour in the pesto and chicken broth. Cover and cook on low for 8 to 10 hours, or until the vegetables have reached the desired tenderness and the flavors have melded. Thirty minutes before serving, stir in the frozen peas and baby spinach. Cover and cook on high until the peas have heated through and the spinach has wilted.

The Verdict

We all really liked this soup, and I loved how many vegetables were hidden throughout. The oil and cheese from the pesto provides a great flavor and texture to this minestrone, making it different from a boring old vegetable soup. Feel free to use whatever vegetables you have on hand (and save the peels and scraps to make homemade vegetable broth, page 300). This soup freezes and reheats very well.

SWEET POTATO AND CHORIZO SOUP

serves 8

The Ingredients

7 cups chicken broth
7 ounces chorizo sausage, sliced
2 large carrots, peeled and chopped
1 large onion, peeled and chopped
1¾ pounds sweet potatoes, peeled and chopped
2 garlic cloves, minced
1 teaspoon curry powder
½ teaspoon crushed red pepper flakes
8 tablespoons sour cream for serving

The Directions

Use a 6-quart slow cooker. Pour in the chicken broth and add the sliced chorizo (no need to brown first). Add the carrots, onion, sweet potatoes, and garlic. Don't worry about how your vegetables look, we're going to blend the soup before serving—just do a coarse chop. Stir in the curry powder and chile flakes.

Cover and cook on low for 6 to 8 hours, or on high for 4 to 5 hours. Before serving, use a hand-held stick blender to blend the soup completely (even the chorizo. I know, it's weird, but trust me). Ladle into bowls and serve with a dollop of sour cream.

The Verdict

Shauna and Danny Ahern adapted this recipe from *Jamie's Food Revolution* by Jamie Oliver. The Aherns write at glutenfreegirl.blogspot.com and porkknifeandspoon.com and are the authors of *Gluten-Free Girl and The Chef*. I was fascinated by the ingredient list, and am so happy that I gave this soup a try in the slow cooker. It's velvety and smooth, with a lot of levels of flavor and spice. It was too fiery for my kids, but Adam and I loved every last drop.

BEANS

Italian White Bean Chili   228

"Real" Pork and Beans   229

Potluck Beans   230

Sweet Potato Chili (Vegan!)   231

ITALIAN WHITE BEAN CHILI

serves 8

The Ingredients

1 pound dry Great Northern white beans
1 pound smoked Italian sausage, sliced (I used turkey)
2 celery stalks, sliced
4 garlic cloves, minced
1/2 teaspoon dried fennel
1/4 teaspoon dried sage
1 (14.5-ounce) can diced tomatoes
2 cups water

The Directions

Use a 6-quart slow cooker. Sort through the beans, and soak overnight. If you don't have time to soak them overnight, boil rapidly on the stovetop for 10 minutes, then remove from the heat and cover. Let the beans sit in hot water for 1 hour before draining and using in the slow cooker.

Put the beans into the cooker, and add the sausage and celery. Add the garlic, fennel, and sage. Pour in the tomatoes and water, and stir to combine. Cover and cook on low for 8 to 10 hours, high for 4 to 5 hours, or until the beans have reached the desired tenderness.

The Verdict

Oh, this is delicious! This is a fantastic white chili—packed full of flavor, but not spicy—perfect for our family. I usually have a package of frozen sausage on hand, and I like that I can create "new" soups simply by changing the variety of sausage.

"REAL" PORK AND BEANS

serves 6

The Ingredients

2 pounds lean pork tenderloin, cut into small cubes

2 (15-ounce) cans of your favorite beans, drained and rinsed (I used kidney)

2 (14.5-ounce) cans diced tomatoes

1 (15-ounce) can corn, drained

1 green bell pepper, seeded and diced

1 onion, peeled and diced

2 tablespoons chili powder

2^1/$_2$ teaspoons cumin

shredded cheese and sour cream as toppings (optional)

The Directions

Put the meat into your slow cooker. Add the beans, and the entire cans of diced tomatoes. Add the drained corn, bell pepper, and onion. Stir in the chili powder and cumin. Cover and cook on low for 8 to 10 hours, or on high for 4 to 6 hours. Serve with shredded cheese and sour cream, if desired.

The Verdict

This is a wonderful soupy chili with a delicious flavor. The pork shreds nicely into the beans, and creates a fantastic smoky flavor along with the cumin. This would be great as an addition to a potluck or to serve to company. Although this is called "pork and beans," it isn't the stuff from a can with the sweet ketchupy flavor. This is much more reminiscent of chili, and makes a fantastic and filling meal.

POTLUCK BEANS

serves 16

The Ingredients

1 pound lean ground meat, browned and drained

1 pound smoked bacon, browned, drained, and diced

1 medium onion, diced and browned

1 cup ketchup (no need to brown!)

¼ cup brown sugar (already brown!)

1 (30-ounce) can pork and beans

1 (15-ounce) can kidney beans, drained and rinsed

1 (15-ounce) can butter beans, drained and rinsed (they look like huge lima beans, and if they aren't in the bean section, try the canned veggie section)

1 tablespoon liquid smoke (yup, it's gluten-free)

The Directions

Use a 6-quart or larger slow cooker. This makes a lot. In a large skillet, brown the ground meat, bacon, and onion. You could probably do this all together, but I did the bacon separately. While the meats and onion are browning, add the rest of the ingredients to the slow cooker. No need to really stir things up quite yet, or the beans will fall apart. Drain the meats well, and dump into the slow cooker. Use a large spoon to gingerly fold in the hot ingredients.

Cover and cook on low for 8 to 10 hours. Stir well and serve to your very best friends.

The Verdict

Our wonderful neighbors, Sandy and Sherman, have been making this bean recipe for a good twenty years to take to family events and potlucks. It's a lovely recipe, and is evidently a bean dish for people who don't even like beans (which I can't imagine. I dream about beans).

SWEET POTATO CHILI (VEGAN!)

serves 4

The Ingredients

2 sweet potatoes, peeled and diced in 2-inch chunks
1 yellow onion, diced
1 red bell pepper, seeded and chopped
1 (14.5-ounce) can tomatoes (whatever's on sale—mine had oregano and roasted garlic)
1 (15-ounce) can red kidney beans, drained and rinsed
2 garlic cloves, minced
1 tablespoon chili powder
1 teaspoon smoked paprika
1 teaspoon chipotle chile powder
1/2 teaspoon kosher salt
1/2 cup orange juice
1 cup water

The Directions

Use a 6-quart slow cooker. Put the sweet potato into the pot. Add the diced onion. Follow with the red bell pepper, tomatoes, beans, garlic, and seasonings. Pour in OJ and water. Cover and cook on low for 6 to 8 hours, or until the onion is translucent and the sweet potato is fork-tender. (If you want the sweet potato to get really squishy and disappear when stirred, cook longer.)

The Verdict

This is a fun and flavorful vegan meal that doesn't leave you hungry fifteen minutes later. I promise.

I loved the sweet smoky flavor, and was thrilled at the depth of flavor that came from this spice combination. The sweet potato and beans were plenty filling, and Adam didn't once mumble that he'd really like a steak. My kids ate it, but unveganized it by adding shredded cheese and sour cream.

SIDE DISHES

RICE

Cheesy Creamed Corn   233

Potatoes au Gruyère   234

Spinach Casserole   235

Stuffing with Apple and Sausage   236

Sun-Dried Tomato Risotto   238

CHEESY CREAMED CORN

serves 8

The Ingredients

2 (16-ounce) packages frozen corn
2 (8-ounce) packages cream cheese
2 tablespoons sugar
2 tablespoons water
4 slices American cheese, crumbled

The Directions

Use a 4-quart slow cooker. Empty the corn packages into your slow cooker. Unwrap the cream cheese and put the blocks on top. Add the sugar, water, and American cheese slice crumbles. Cover and cook on low for 6 hours. Stir well before serving.

The Verdict

I ate way way way way way too much of this. I just couldn't stop. This is absolutely delicious, and you really should make it right away. And then go to the gym.

POTATOES AU GRUYÈRE

serves 8

The Ingredients

2 tablespoons butter
6 large russet potatoes, peeled and sliced super thin (1/8 inch)
1 teaspoon ground nutmeg
2 teaspoons kosher salt
1 teaspoon black pepper
8 ounces Gruyère cheese, grated
2 cups heavy cream

The Directions

Use a 6-quart slow cooker. Butter the inside of your stoneware insert. Put one third of the very thinly sliced potatoes (if you have a mandoline, now is the time to use it!) in the bottom of your cooker. In a small bowl, combine the nutmeg, salt, and pepper. Sprinkle a large pinch of this seasoning blend all over the potatoes. Add a handful of cheese. Pour 1/4 cup heavy cream on top. Repeat the layers until you run out of ingredients. Finish with the rest of the cream.

Your cooker will be about half full. Cover and cook on high for 3 to 4 hours, or until the potatoes are fork-tender. Leave the lid off during the last 20 minutes of cooking.

The Verdict

In our family, these are called "Aunt Jeanne's" potatoes. We are lucky enough to enjoy these potatoes during almost every holiday dinner, and we love them. Everyone does. They smell delicious while cooking, and taste even better.

SPINACH CASSEROLE

serves 8 to 10

The Ingredients
cooking spray
3 (10-ounce) packages frozen spinach, thawed and drained
2 cups cottage cheese
1½ cups shredded mozzarella cheese
3 eggs, lightly beaten
¼ cup all-purpose flour (I used a gluten-free baking mix)
1 teaspoon kosher salt

The Directions
Use a 2-quart slow cooker. Spray the stoneware insert well with cooking spray. Squeeze any remaining water out of the frozen spinach and place in a large mixing bowl. Add the cottage and mozzarella cheeses, eggs, flour, and salt. Mix together with a spoon until the ingredients are combined. Pour into the prepared slow cooker. Cover and cook on high for 3 to 4 hours, or until the top has begun to brown and the casserole pulls away from the sides. Let cook on high for an additional 20 minutes with the lid off to release condensation.

The Verdict
Popeye would be so proud. This is a fabulous spinach recipe—rich and creamy and absolutely delicious.

STUFFING WITH APPLE AND SAUSAGE

serves 8

The Ingredients

12 cups dried bread cubes (I used a loaf of brown rice bread)

8 ounces ground pork or turkey sausage, browned and drained

3 tablespoons butter, melted

1½ cups chopped Granny Smith apples (no need to peel)

1½ cups chopped onion

1½ cups diced celery

1½ teaspoons rubbed sage

1 teaspoon kosher salt

½ teaspoon pepper

½ cup chicken broth, plus an additional ¼ cup if desired

The Directions

Use a 6-quart slow cooker. Cut the bread into ½-inch cubes and bake at 350°F for 20 minutes, flipping once, or until the bread is golden brown and toasty. While the bread is toasting, brown the sausage on the stovetop and drain. Toss the bread cubes and sausage together in your slow cooker, and pour in the melted butter.

Add the apples, vegetables, and seasonings. Use two large spoons to toss the ingredients and disperse the spices. Pour in ½ cup chicken broth, and stir gingerly to coat the bread and vegetables with the broth. Cover and cook on high for 2 to 3 hours. When done the bread will have browned on the top and edges, and the vegetables will be tender. Stir well, and add an additional ¼ cup chicken broth if you'd like added moisture.

The Verdict

I can easily eat a bowlful of stuffing for dinner and forget about dinner. The apple and sausage wake up this stuffing, and create great flavor and moistness. I was worried when we first went gluten-free that we'd no longer be able to enjoy good stuffing, and I'm happy to report I was wrong. Very wrong. Skip the boxed stuff, and make your own stuffing this holiday season!

SUN-DRIED TOMATO RISOTTO

serves 4

The Ingredients

1/2 cup sun-dried tomatoes in oil
1 1/2 cups Arborio rice (in a box in the rice aisle)
4 cups chicken broth
1/2 cup shredded Swiss cheese (to add later)

The Directions

Use a 4-quart slow cooker. Put the sun-dried tomatoes into the bottom of your slow cooker. Add the rice and swirl it around in the tomatoes until the rice is coated with oil. Add the chicken broth. Cover and cook on high for 2 to 4 hours, or until the rice is tender. Remove the lid and stir in the Swiss cheese. Turn off the cooker and let the risotto sit in the slow cooker for 10 minutes with the lid off before serving.

The Verdict

This risotto is creamy and luscious, with a fabulous flavor. I was once told by a chef that "real" risotto doesn't use Swiss cheese, only grated Parmesan. I'm glad I had already made this a few times before I heard this, because I might not have experimented otherwise. This is one of my favorite side dishes—it's absolute comfort food.

FISH

Italian Catfish   *240*

Salmon with Lime Butter   *241*

ITALIAN CATFISH

serves 4

The Ingredients

aluminum foil
4 catfish fillets
1 tablespoon Italian seasoning
$1/2$ teaspoon kosher salt
$1/4$ teaspoon ground black pepper
1 red bell pepper, seeded and sliced
1 green bell pepper, seeded and sliced
1 small yellow onion, peeled and sliced in rings
2 tablespoons butter, cut in thin strips

The Directions

Use a 6-quart slow cooker. Lay a length of foil out on your kitchen countertop. Place the fish fillets in the center. Sprinkle on the Italian seasoning, salt, and pepper. Add the peppers and onion. Arrange the slices of butter on top of the vegetables. Fold the foil over and crimp the sides to make a packet. Place in an empty slow cooker (do not add water) and cover. Cook for 2 hours on high, or until the fish flakes easily with a fork.

The Verdict

È squisito, buon appetito!

SALMON WITH LIME BUTTER

serves 2

The Ingredients

aluminum foil
2 salmon fillets
1 tablespoon butter, melted
$1/2$ tablespoon lime juice
$1/8$ teaspoon kosher salt
$1/8$ teaspoon black pepper
$1/2$ teaspoon dried minced parsley
2 garlic cloves, minced

The Directions

Use a 4-quart slow cooker. Spread a length of foil out on your countertop, and place the fish in the middle. In a small bowl, combine the butter, lime juice, salt, pepper, parsley, and garlic. Brush the butter and lime mixture on the fish with a pastry brush. Fold the foil over and crimp the sides to create an enclosed packet. Place the packet into an empty slow cooker and cover. Cook on high for 2 hours, or until the fish flakes easily with a fork.

The Verdict

We eat a lot of salmon, and I'm so glad to have another way to season it. This has a nice mild citrus flavor with a hint of buttery goodness. Yum. Serve with fresh veggies and rice or potatoes.

POULTRY

Baked Chicken with Feta & Fennel   243

Chicken Korma   244

Country Captain   245

Creamy Turkey and Green Beans   247

Ginger Almond Chicken   248

Pad Thai   249

Sweet Garlic Barbecue Chicken   251

White Wine Coq au Vin   252

BAKED CHICKEN WITH FETA & FENNEL

serves 6

The Ingredients

1 (5-pound) whole chicken
³/₄ teaspoon kosher salt
¹/₈ teaspoon pepper
3 garlic cloves, minced
1 tablespoon dried oregano
1 fennel bulb, trimmed, cored, and sliced
2 lemons, juiced
³/₄ cup pitted kalamata olives, drained
¹/₃ cup crumbled feta cheese (to add later)

The Directions

Use a 6-quart slow cooker. Skin the chicken the best you can using poultry shears. Remove and discard the neck and giblets. In a tiny bowl, combine the salt, pepper, garlic, and oregano. Rub the spice mixture all over the chicken, inside and out. Put the chicken into your slow cooker. Nestle pieces of fennel around the chicken. Squeeze on the lemon juice and dump in the olives. Cover and cook on low for 7 to 8 hours, or on high for 4 to 5 hours. Check the internal temperature with a meat thermometer to ensure doneness (165°F). The meat should be quite tender and fall off the bones easily. Sprinkle the feta onto each serving.

The Verdict

I was initially concerned that the chicken would taste like licorice, because the scent of the fennel was so strong while I was cutting it. I shouldn't have worried. The flavor of the fennel was mild, like a cross between an onion and celery. The kalamata olives and lemon juice provide an excellent flavor to the meat. This is delicious chicken. Remember to save the carcass to make homemade broth (see page 294)!

CHICKEN KORMA

serves 4

The Ingredients

1 pound boneless, skinless chicken, cut in chunks (I prefer thighs)
1 large potato, peeled and cut in $1/2$-inch chunks
1 large onion, coarsely chopped
1 (14.5-ounce) can stewed tomatoes and juice
1 garlic clove, minced
1 teaspoon curry powder
$1/2$ teaspoon dried ginger
$1/4$ teaspoon ground cloves
1 teaspoon kosher salt
1 cinnamon stick
$1/2$ cup sour cream or plain yogurt (to add later)
cooked white or brown basmati rice for serving

The Directions

Use a 4-quart slow cooker. Put the chicken in the bottom of your slow cooker. Add the potato and onion. Pour in the stewed tomatoes, and add the garlic and spices. Cover and cook on low for 6 to 8 hours, or on high for 4 hours. Discard the cinnamon stick, and stir in the sour cream or yogurt. Serve over white or brown basmati rice.

The Verdict

Delicious, absolutely delicious. My family really likes Indian food, and before I did my "year of slow cooking" challenge, we'd order it once a week for delivery. I'm thrilled to say that we no longer have this tradition, and instead make korma in the slow cooker, saving an awful lot of money.

COUNTRY CAPTAIN

serves 6

The Ingredients

1³/4 pounds boneless, skinless chicken thighs
2 Granny Smith apples, peeled, cored, and diced
1 onion, peeled and diced
1 green bell pepper, seeded and diced
3 garlic cloves, minced
1 tablespoon curry powder
1 teaspoon ground ginger
¹/2 teaspoon kosher salt
¹/4 teaspoon cayenne pepper
¹/4 cup raisins
1 (14.5-ounce) can diced tomatoes
¹/2 cup chicken broth
1 cup raw long-grain basmati white rice (to add later)
1 pound large fully cooked shrimp (frozen is fine, to add later)

The Directions

Use a 6-quart slow cooker. There are a lot of ingredients, but this goes together fast and I promise it will be worth the effort! Put the chicken into the bottom of your stoneware. Add the apples, onion, and bell pepper. Add the garlic and all the spices. Toss in the raisins and tomatoes. Stir in the chicken broth. Cover and cook on low for 6 to 7 hours, or until the chicken is tender but still intact. Remove the chicken carefully from the slow cooker, and place in a covered container to keep warm. Stir in raw white rice. Cover again and cook on high for about 30 minutes, or until the rice is bite-tender. Stir in frozen shrimp, re-cover, and cook for another 10 to 15 minutes, or until the shrimp are heated through. Serve the rice and shrimp mixture on a plate with the chicken pieces arranged on top.

(CONTINUED)

The Verdict

I had never before heard of country captain chicken until I saw a *Throwdown with Bobby Flay* on the Food Network, which featured this dish. I immediately started Googling recipes before settling on a compilation. I was thrilled at the results. Bobby, dig out your slow cooker—this is a winner.

The shrimp is the most expensive component in this recipe, and while delicious, it isn't absolutely necessary. You can still have a fabulous dinner if you decide to omit the shrimp.

CREAMY TURKEY AND GREEN BEANS

serves 6

The Ingredients

2 pounds turkey breast, cut in chunks
1/2 cup beef broth
2 tablespoons balsamic vinegar
1 onion, thinly sliced
8 ounces sliced mushrooms
1 tablespoon dried parsley
1/2 cup half-and-half or heavy cream (to add later)
1 cup frozen green beans (to add later)
cooked pasta for serving

The Directions

Use a 4-quart slow cooker. Put the turkey into the bottom of your slow cooker. Add the beef broth and balsamic vinegar. Put the onion, mushrooms, and parsley into the pot and stir to combine. Cover and cook on low for 6 to 7 hours, or on high for about 4 hours. Stir in the cream and green beans. Cover and cook on high for another 30 minutes, or until the beans are thawed and heated through. Serve over cooked pasta.

The Verdict

The kids wanted me to call this "Winner Winner Turkey Dinner," and maybe I should have. It's a great meal.

GINGER ALMOND CHICKEN

serves 4

The Ingredients

2 pounds boneless, skinless chicken thighs
1 onion, peeled and sliced in rings
1 teaspoon dried ginger
½ cup teriyaki sauce (La Choy and Tamari wheat-free brands are gluten-free)
3 green onions, sliced
1 (16-ounce) package frozen stir-fry vegetables (to add later)
cooked white basmati rice for serving
¼ cup sliced almonds (to sprinkle over the top after cooking)

The Directions

Use a 4-quart slow cooker. Put the chicken into the bottom of the slow cooker. Add the onion rings, ginger, teriyaki sauce, and green onions. Toss the chicken and onions to coat evenly with the sauce and ginger. Cover and cook on low for 6 hours, or on high for 3 to 4 hours. Add the stir-fry vegetables and cook on high for 30 to 40 minutes, or until fully hot. Serve over white basmati rice with 1 tablespoon sliced almonds as a garnish per plate.

The Verdict

This is a great recipe to throw together when you're craving Chinese takeout or delivery. All of us thoroughly enjoyed our meal, and my brother and sister-in-law enjoyed the leftovers.

PAD THAI

serves 6

The Ingredients

1½ pounds boneless, skinless chicken thighs, cut in 1-inch pieces
1 (8-ounce) can bamboo shoots, drained
4 garlic cloves, chopped
3 green onions, sliced
1 red bell pepper, seeded and sliced
1 tablespoon Asian chili paste (Sambal Oelek)
½ teaspoon grated lime zest
2 tablespoons lime juice
4 tablespoons fish sauce
2 tablespoons brown sugar
2 tablespoons rice wine vinegar
1 (14-ounce) package Thai Kitchen® pad thai rice noodles
2 tablespoons chopped fresh cilantro (optional)
soy sauce for serving

The Directions

Use a 6-quart slow cooker. Put the chicken into the bottom of your slow cooker, and add the bamboo shoots, garlic, and vegetables. In a mixing bowl, mix together the sauce ingredients: chili paste, lime zest, lime juice, fish sauce, brown sugar, and rice wine vinegar. Pour evenly over the top.

Cover and cook on low for 6 to 8 hours, or on high for about 4 hours. Cook the rice noodles according to package instructions, drain, and toss with the contents from the slow cooker. Add chopped cilantro if you'd like. Serve with a bit of gluten-free soy sauce at the table.

(CONTINUED)

The Verdict

Making Pad Thai at home is easy and inexpensive. Skip the takeout and make this instead on DVD night. If you bought fish sauce and chili sauce for this recipe, you can use them both again for the Meatballs in Peanut Chili Sauce on page 214.

SWEET GARLIC BARBECUE CHICKEN

serves 4

The Ingredients

1½ pounds boneless, skinless chicken pieces
1 (14.5-ounce) can diced tomatoes, undrained
2 onions, coarsely chopped
1 head garlic, cloves peeled and intact (about 15 cloves)
3 tablespoons brown sugar
1 tablespoon gluten-free Worcestershire sauce
cooked pasta or rice for serving

The Directions

Use a 4-quart slow cooker. Put the chicken into the bottom of your slow cooker. Add the tomatoes and chopped onion. Add the garlic cloves, brown sugar, and Worcestershire sauce. Cover and cook on low for 8 to 10 hours, or on high for 5 to 6 hours. Serve over gluten-free pasta or rice.

The Verdict

This has an amazing flavor. I seem to always have the ingredients in the house for this recipe, and I'm so glad! It's extraordinary.

WHITE WINE COQ AU VIN

serves 4

The Ingredients

1½ pounds boneless, skinless chicken thighs

4 strips bacon (¼ pound), chopped

1 medium onion, sliced into rings

½ teaspoon black pepper

1 teaspoon herbes de Provence (homemade recipe on page 169)

1½ cups baby carrots

3 celery stalks, chopped

1 cup dry white wine (I used Chardonnay)

½ cup chicken broth

The Directions

Use a 6-quart slow cooker. Put the chicken into the bottom of your slow cooker (frozen is fine). Add the chopped bacon and onion to the meat. Add the pepper and herbes de Provence. Toss in the carrots and celery. Pour in the wine and broth. Cover and cook on low for 6 to 8 hours, high for 4 to 5, or until the vegetables have reached the desired tenderness. Serve in a wide-mouthed bowl with crusty bread (I use rolls made from a gluten-free bread mix) for dunking, and a leafy garden salad.

The Verdict

This is a light twist on the classic French dish. I like the lightness the Chardonnay provides, and prefer this version. The smoky flavor from the bacon is pronounced, and pairs well with the salty chicken broth. If you already have a bottle of red wine open or prefer a heartier dish, simply swap wines. I buy the little airline-size bottles of wine for cooking.

BEEF, PORK, LAMB & VENISON

American Chop Suey   254

Apricot-Glazed Pork Roast   255

Asian Shredded Beef   256

Beef Bourguignon   258

Dijon Corned Beef   260

Hawaiian Barbecue Ribs   261

Honey-Glazed Ham with Thyme   262

Leg of Lamb with Rosemary and Lemon   263

Loose Meat Sandwiches   264

Mushroom Pork Chops   265

Old-Fashioned Pot Roast   266

Orange Beef   267

Peanut Butter Indonesian Pork   268

Puffy Pizza Casserole   269

Pulled Pork with Sauerkraut   271

Ravioli Lasagna*   272

Snowy Day Ribs   273

Spicy Pineapple Chops   274

Taco Lasagna   275

Teriyaki and Apricot Chops   276

Tex-Mex Pot Roast   277

Thai Beef   278

Venison Roast   279

* Gluten-free ravioli are terribly expensive compared to traditional frozen ravioli. If you do not need to worry about gluten, this would be an under-$7 meal for you.

AMERICAN CHOP SUEY
(MACARONI AND BEEF)

serves 6

The Ingredients

1 pound lean ground beef, browned and drained

5 bacon strips, diced

1 large onion, diced

1 green bell pepper, seeded and diced

1 (14.5-ounce) can diced tomatoes

1 can water

6 garlic cloves, chopped

1 (26-ounce) jar prepared pasta sauce

1 (16-ounce) package elbow macaroni (I used brown rice pasta)

1 cup shredded cheddar cheese (optional)

The Directions

Use a 6-quart slow cooker. In a large skillet, brown the beef, bacon, and onion. When the meat is no longer pink, drain well and put the skillet contents in your slow cooker. Add the pepper, tomatoes, water, garlic, and pasta sauce, and stir well to combine. Cover and cook on low for 6 to 8 hours, or on high for about 4 hours. Stir in raw pasta and cover again. Cook on high for about 30 minutes, or until the pasta is bite-tender. Top with shredded cheese, if desired.

The Verdict

This recipe was sent to me by Amy Jo, who first learned about American chop suey on an episode of *Diners, Drive-Ins, and Dives* on the Food Network. The name is regional, and (according to Wikipedia) comes from New England. Amy Jo makes this once a month for her boys. My friend Lorraine's four daughters loved it, and so did my girls.

APRICOT-GLAZED PORK ROAST

serves 4

The Ingredients

2 pounds boneless pork shoulder roast

1 (18-ounce) jar apricot jam

1 onion, chopped

2 tablespoons prepared Dijon mustard

1/4 cup chicken broth

The Directions

Use a 4-quart slow cooker. Place the meat into the bottom of your cooker. Add the jam, onion, and mustard. Flip the pork over a few times to distribute the onion and mix the sauce. Pour the chicken broth over the top and cover. Cook on low for 8 hours, or on high for about 4 hours. Your meat is done when it has reached the desired tenderness. Slice and serve with a spoonful of sauce from the pot.

The Verdict

This is a fantastic simple recipe. The Dijon cuts the sweetness of the jam nicely. If you'd like a thicker glaze, scoop out the juice from the crock and simmer on the stovetop in a saucepan until reduced.

ASIAN SHREDDED BEEF

serves 8

The Ingredients

4 pounds boneless beef or pork roast

2 teaspoons Chinese five-spice powder (sold in bottles, or make your own with the recipe below)

2 teaspoons garlic powder (or 6 garlic cloves, minced)

6 tablespoons ketchup

6 tablespoons honey

1/2 cup gluten-free soy sauce

1/2 cup gluten-free hoisin sauce

cooked white or brown basmati rice or shredded cabbage (optional)

CHINESE FIVE-SPICE POWDER

1 teaspoon ground cinnamon

1 teaspoon crushed anise seed

1/4 teaspoon ground fennel

1/4 teaspoon ground black pepper

1/8 teaspoon ground cloves

Mix the spices well and store in an airtight container for up to 6 months

The Directions

Use a 6-quart slow cooker. Trim any visible fat from the meat, and plop it into your stoneware. Sprinkle the dried spices directly onto the meat, and top with the ketchup and honey. Pour in the soy and hoisin sauces. Cover and cook on low for 8 to 9 hours, or until the meat shreds easily with a fork. You may need to take the meat out and cut it in chunks after 8 hours, then turn to high for an hour or so to get it to shred nicely (I did this).

Serve over white or brown basmati rice or shredded cabbage. I used the cabbage, and we all liked it. The cabbage provided a bit of a crunch at first, but then it got warm and soggy with the sauce. I liked it better when it was soggy—if I was making this just for myself, I'd pour the bag of cabbage into the pot to make it wilted, but the rest of the family prefers the crunch.

The Verdict

We all really liked this meal. The kids ate a ton of the beef, and continued to eat cold pieces later in the night after dinner. The flavor is tangy with a slightly sweet taste. If you would like some heat, you can add whole peppers to the pot while it's cooking or some red pepper flakes. Thank you to Christin, who wrote to me through my Web site, for this recipe.

BEEF BOURGUIGNON
serves 6

The Ingredients

2 tablespoons olive oil

6 bacon strips—no need to cook (I used turkey)

1 onion, sliced in rings

4 garlic cloves, smashed and chopped

3 pounds beef roast, cut in chunks, or beef stew meat

1 tablespoon herbes de Provence (purchased or homemade, page 169)

1 teaspoon kosher salt

1/2 teaspoon black pepper

1 tablespoon tomato paste

1 cup carrots (chopped or baby, your choice)

2 cups red wine (you can use nonalcoholic if you wish)

whipped mashed potatoes for serving

The Directions

Use a 6-quart slow cooker. In the bottom of your stoneware, smear around the olive oil. Then lay down 3 strips of bacon. Add the sliced onion and garlic. Put the meat into the pot on top of the onion and garlic, and sprinkle on the dried spices and herbs. Toss the meat to distribute the spices to all sides. Add the tomato paste. Lay the other 3 strips of bacon on top of the meat, and throw in the carrots. Pour the wine over the whole thing.

Cover and let cook on low for 8 to 9 hours, high for 4 to 5 hours, or until the meat has reached the desired tenderness. Serve with whipped mashed potatoes and a ladleful of the crock juices.

The Verdict

This is an easy copycat (or sort of copycat) of Julia Child's famous Beef Bourguignon. I cut the butter completely, and simplified the spices, but the flavor is all there.

The kids weren't crazy about the carrots, because they took on the wine flavor and were a bit tart, but Adam and I loved them. This is a companyworthy meal, and has been very well reviewed on my Web site.

DIJON CORNED BEEF

serves 6

The Ingredients

3 pounds corned beef, trimmed of fat
1 tablespoon honey
2 tablespoons brown sugar
1 tablespoon prepared Dijon mustard
10 whole cloves (or ½ teaspoon ground cloves)

The Directions

Use a 6-quart slow cooker. Put the meat into your slow cooker, and discard the inserted flavor packet (keep it to use in a different recipe). In a small bowl, make a paste of the honey, brown sugar, mustard, and cloves. Rub the mixture on all sides of the meat. Cover and cook on low for 8 to 10 hours, or on high for 4 to 5 hours. The meat will be quite tender and juicy, and cut easily with a fork.

The Verdict

I really should make corned beef more often, not only on St. Patrick's Day. I prefer my vegetables cooked separately from the corned beef, but feel free to load potato, cabbage wedges, and carrots into the crock along with the meat.

HAWAIIAN BARBECUE RIBS

serves 4

The Ingredients

2 pounds boneless beef short ribs
1/3 cup gluten-free soy sauce
2 tablespoons brown sugar
1 tablespoon honey
1/2 teaspoon Chinese five-spice powder (you can make your own with the recipe on page 256)
6 garlic cloves, minced

The Directions

Use a 4-quart slow cooker. Put the ribs into your slow cooker, and top with the soy sauce, brown sugar, honey and five-spice powder. Stir in the garlic. Cover and cook on low for 6 to 8 hours, or on high for 4 to 5 hours. Your meat will become more tender if cooked on low for a long period of time.

The Verdict

These ribs are fantastic. I served them with corn on the cob and a large green salad. This is what ribs should taste like: tender, juicy, sticky, and sweet.

HONEY-GLAZED HAM WITH THYME

serves 6

The Ingredients

1 (5- to 7-pound) bone-in, spiral cut ham
¼ cup apple cider vinegar
¼ cup honey
¼ cup butter, melted
1 teaspoon gluten-free Worcestershire sauce
1 tablespoon brown sugar
2 teaspoons ground thyme

The Directions

Use a 6-quart slow cooker. Unwrap the ham and discard the flavor packet. Put the ham into the slow cooker. In a small bowl, combine the vinegar, honey, butter, Worcestershire sauce, brown sugar, and thyme. Pour the mixture evenly over the ham. Cover and cook on low for 6 hours, or until heated through.

The Verdict

Oh, yum. Slow-cooked ham is super easy, and it always comes out fantastic. The meat stays perfectly moist without needing to baste, and it tastes wonderful. My family really likes this glaze—it's sweet, but not over the top.

LEG OF LAMB WITH
ROSEMARY AND LEMON

serves 8

The Ingredients
1/4 cup honey
2 tablespoons prepared Dijon mustard
1 tablespoon dried rosemary
1 teaspoon black pepper
1 teaspoon kosher salt
1 teaspoon lemon zest
2 tablespoons fresh lemon juice (1 lemon, juiced)
3 pounds whole leg of lamb

The Directions
Use a 4-quart slow cooker. In a small bowl, combine the honey, mustard, spices, lemon zest, and lemon juice. Stir with a spoon to form a paste. Smear this paste on all sides of the lamb roast. Cover and cook on low for 8 hours, or on high for 4 to 5 hours. You can check the doneness with a meat thermometer, if you'd like, but I usually cook until it's super tender and I can cut it with a fork. If your meat isn't as moist/tender as you'd like, you can cut it in half or in chunks and return it to the pot to soak up more moisture. I don't like dry lamb.

The Verdict
I really liked this, and so did the twelve people in my family who enjoyed some at a family dinner. The flavor of the rub is fantastic, and the drippings make a wonderful gravy.

Serve with mashed potatoes and a big side of your favorite vegetables. Baa!

Lamb is a seasonal meat, and is the least expensive and easiest to find in the early Spring. When on sale, buy lots to store in the freezer to enjoy year-round.

LOOSE MEAT SANDWICHES

serves 8

The Ingredients

1 pound extra-lean ground beef or turkey

1 onion, finely diced

1 teaspoon kosher salt

1 tablespoon garlic powder

1 tablespoon sugar

1 tablespoon prepared mustard

1 tablespoon apple cider vinegar

2 cups beef broth

8 hamburger buns (I used gluten-free bread, toasted)

hamburger fixin's: pickles, lettuce, sliced tomato, additional mustard

The Directions

Use a 6-quart slow cooker. Crumble the ground meat into your slow cooker. Add the onion, dry spices, and sugar. Add the prepared mustard and apple cider vinegar. Pour in 1 cup of beef broth, and stir the contents of the cooker very well. Pour in the other cup of broth and cover. Cook on low for 8 to 10 hours. Stir well before serving and scoop onto hamburger buns. Top with the desired fixin's.

The Verdict

Our family friend, Harvey Althaus, asked if I had made Loose Meat Sandwiches in the slow cooker, and I hadn't. My only experience with these sandwiches came from Roseanne Connor's Loose Meat restaurant on the TV show *Roseanne*. These are delicious. The meat is sweet and garlicky, and tastes incredible with a bunch of mustard. This is a new family favorite—thanks, Harvey!

MUSHROOM PORK CHOPS

serves 4

The Ingredients

1 onion, sliced into rings
4 pork chops
1 teaspoon garlic powder
$1/4$ teaspoon pepper
8 ounces sliced mushrooms

CREAMY TOPPING

1 tablespoon butter
3 tablespoons all-purpose flour (I used a gluten-free baking mix)
$1/2$ cup low-fat milk
$1/2$ cup chicken broth

The Directions

Use a 4-quart slow cooker. Place the sliced onion into the bottom of your cooker, separated into rings. Place the pork chops on top. Sprinkle the garlic powder and pepper onto the chops. Add the mushrooms. Make a roux on the stovetop by melting the butter in a skillet over low heat. Whisk the flour into the melted butter, and slowly add the milk and chicken broth. When fully combined and no lumps remain, pour evenly on top of the mushrooms and chops.

Cover and cook on low for 6 to 8 hours, or until the chops are thoroughly cooked and have reached the desired tenderness.

The Verdict

I served this with a big pile of mashed potatoes and some frozen string beans, and Adam and the kids were super happy. Pork chops are a very versatile cut of meat, and don't have a very distinct flavor on their own. Instead, they're chameleon-like and take on whatever flavor you season them with.

OLD-FASHIONED POT ROAST

serves 6 to 8

The Ingredients

4 pounds beef roast (chuck or rump)
2 tablespoons flour (I used a gluten-free baking mix)
1 teaspoon kosher salt
$\frac{1}{2}$ teaspoon black pepper
2 teaspoons garlic powder
1 tablespoon olive oil
1 medium onion, sliced in rings
2 large russet potatoes, cut in 2-inch chunks
1 cup baby carrots
1 cup sliced celery
3 tablespoons gluten-free Worcestershire sauce
$\frac{1}{2}$ cup beef broth

The Directions

Use a 6-quart slow cooker. In a plastic zippered bag, shake thawed beef roast with the flour, salt, pepper, and garlic powder. Remove the roast from the bag, and brown all sides in a large skillet with the olive oil on the stovetop. While the meat is browning, place the sliced onion in the bottom of your slow cooker. Add the browned meat, and toss in the potatoes, carrots, and celery. Pour the Worcestershire sauce and beef broth on top. Cover and cook on low for 8 to 10 hours. If your meat isn't as moist as you'd like, cut it in half and return it to the pot for another hour to soak in more juices.

The Verdict

This is what pot roast should taste like! If you'd prefer to skip browning the meat on the stove, you may—I've done it both ways. The browning provides a nice color, flavor, and texture to the meat that's noticeable but not necessary to achieve good results.

ORANGE BEEF

serves 4

The Ingredients

1½ pounds beef round steak, sliced or beef stir-fry strips
¼ cup gluten-free soy sauce
2 teaspoons ground ginger
3 tablespoons honey
½ cup orange juice
1 red bell pepper, seeded and sliced
1 green bell pepper, seeded and sliced
6 green onions, sliced
1 small head bok choy, cut in 1-inch chunks
cooked white rice for serving

The Directions

Use a 4-quart slow cooker. Marinate the meat in a plastic zippered bag overnight in the soy sauce, ginger, honey, and orange juice. In the morning, pour the contents of the bag into your slow cooker. Add the vegetables on top of the meat. Cover and cook on low for 6 to 7 hours, or on high for 3 to 4 hours. Serve over white rice.

The Verdict

Your take-out cravings will be satisfied with this meal! My kids refused to try the bok choy but ate the rest of their meal without complaint, which means they liked it. If you'd like, you can add a kick with some dried red pepper flakes at the table.

PEANUT BUTTER INDONESIAN PORK

serves 6

The Ingredients

3 pounds pork loin
½ cup gluten-free soy sauce
½ cup peanut butter (creamy or chunky, your choice)
2 garlic cloves, chopped
½ teaspoon crushed red pepper flakes
1 (8-ounce) can crushed pineapple
cooked rice for serving

The Directions

Use a 6-quart slow cooker. Place the meat into the bottom of your slow cooker (frozen is just fine). In a mixing bowl, combine the soy sauce, peanut butter, garlic, red pepper flakes, and the whole can of pineapple. Stir well, and pour over the top of the meat. Cover and cook on low for 8 to 10 hours, or until the pork is tender enough to pull apart with a fork. Serve over rice with sauce from the pot.

The Verdict

I hadn't paired peanut butter and pineapple together before trying it out on this dish, and I really liked the results. I like using chunky peanut butter for an added element of texture, but many of my readers prefer the smoothness of creamy peanut butter. This is a great way to eat pork.

PUFFY PIZZA CASSEROLE

serves 8

The Ingredients

1 pound lean ground beef

1 small onion, diced

1 garlic clove, minced

1 (1.5-ounce) packet spaghetti sauce mix (if using store-bought, look out for hidden gluten. You can make your own with the recipe below)

½ teaspoon dried oregano

1 (15-ounce) can tomato sauce

½ cup water

FOR PUFFY TOPPING

1 cup all-purpose flour (I used Pamela's Baking Mix)

1 cup milk

2 eggs

1 cup shredded mozzarella cheese

20 pepperoni slices

sliced peppers or mushrooms as pizza toppings (optional)

HOMEMADE SPAGHETTI SAUCE MIX

makes 1 packet

1½ teaspoons kosher salt

1 tablespoon cornstarch

1 tablespoon dried minced onion

1 tablespoon dried parsley flakes

(CONTINUED)

1 teaspoon sugar
¼ teaspoon garlic powder
2 teaspoons green pepper flakes
¾ teaspoon Italian seasoning

Mix ingredients together and use in lieu of a store-bought packet.

The Directions

Use a 4-quart slow cooker. In a very large skillet, brown the beef, onion, and garlic on the stovetop. Drain the fat, and add the spaghetti sauce mix, oregano, tomato sauce, and water. Stir over low heat until tiny bubbles appear. Remove from the heat and scoop into the slow cooker. In a mixing bowl, combine the flour, milk, eggs, and cheese. Pour evenly over the top. Place the pepperoni slices on top of the topping.

Cover and cook on high for 4 hours, or until the topping has turned golden brown, puffed up, and pulled away from the sides.

The Verdict

I was given this recipe from a friend of mine, and was eager to give it a try. I'm so glad I did! The casserole puffs up beautifully, and satisfies any cravings you may have without worrying about tipping the pizza guy.

PULLED PORK WITH SAUERKRAUT

serves 8

The Ingredients

2 pounds pork tenderloin
1/2 teaspoon dry mustard
1 teaspoon dried thyme
1 teaspoon dried sage
2 teaspoons paprika
1 teaspoon kosher salt
1 teaspoon black pepper
1/2 cup shredded carrot
1 (14.5-ounce) can sauerkraut
1 teaspoon caraway seeds
8 rolls for serving (optional)

The Directions

Use a 6-quart slow cooker. Put the roast into the bottom of your slow cooker. In a mixing bowl, combine the mustard, thyme, sage, paprika, salt, and pepper. Rub the dry spices on all sides of the roast. Put the shredded carrot, sauerkraut, and caraway seeds into the empty mixing bowl, and stir to combine. Pour over the top of the meat. Cover and cook on low for 8 to 10 hours, or until the meat shreds easily with two forks. Shred completely and serve as is or spooned into toasted rolls (I like to make my own from a package of gluten-free bread mix).

The Verdict

I love the way the tang from the sauerkraut tastes mixed with the seasoned pork. Adam had his pork on a roll with a lot of mustard, and the girls and I ate ours plain in a bowl. If you're trying to sneak extra vegetables into your dinners, this is a great way to do so. Add some shredded zucchini or cucumber—no one will ever know it's in there.

RAVIOLI LASAGNA

serves 6

The Ingredients

1 pound lean ground beef, browned and drained

1 (28-ounce) jar prepared pasta sauce

25 to 30 frozen cheese or meat ravioli (Conte's brand has gluten-free ravioli: contespasta.com)

2 cups Italian blend shredded cheese

2 tablespoons warm water

The Directions

Use a 4-quart slow cooker. In a large skillet on the stovetop, brown the ground beef. Drain well, add the contents of a jar of pasta sauce (retain the jar!), and stir to combine. Scoop a spoonful of the meat mixture into the bottom of an empty slow cooker. Add a layer of frozen ravioli. Add more meat mixture, then another layer of ravioli. Continue layering until the meat and ravioli have been used. Top with the shredded cheese. Put the warm water into the empty sauce jar and shake. Pour the tomatoey liquid evenly over the top.

Cover and cook on low for 6 hours, or on high for 3 to 4 hours. Your lasagna is done when the pasta on the ravioli is tender and the filling is heated through.

The Verdict

If you are not gluten-free, this will be much less expensive than it would be if using gluten-free ravioli, which are quite costly. (My mom calls them "little diamonds.") This is such an easy way to make lasagna. Feel free to throw in a layer or two of spinach or mushrooms, and use homemade marinara sauce (page 298).

SNOWY DAY RIBS

serves 4

The Ingredients

2 pounds boneless beef short ribs
1/2 cup each: crushed tomatoes, apple butter, and whole berry cranberry sauce
mashed or baked potatoes for serving

The Directions

Use a 4-quart slow cooker. Put the ribs into your slow cooker, and top with the tomatoes, apple butter, and cranberry sauce. Cover and cook on low for 8 hours, or on high for 4 hours. Serve with mashed or baked potatoes.

The Verdict

This recipe came from one of my readers, Shari, who calls them her "snow day ribs." They are sweet and succulent—the meat shreds apart nicely and tastes fantastic. We all loved our dinner. Canned cranberry sauce goes on sale during the winter months, and many times you can find cans for less than $1. Stock up during this time to enjoy throughout the year.

SPICY PINEAPPLE CHOPS

serves 4

The Ingredients

4 pork chops
$1/4$ cup pineapple juice
2 tablespoons brown sugar
1 tablespoon Tabasco sauce

The Directions

Use a 4-quart slow cooker. Put the chops into the bottom of your slow cooker. Pour on the pineapple juice, and add the brown sugar and Tabasco sauce. Flip the chops over a few times to allow the liquid to get on all sides. Cover and cook on low for 6 to 8 hours, or until the chops are thoroughly cooked and have reached the desired tenderness.

The Verdict

I made this up on a stormy day when I couldn't leave the house. We had some frostbitten chops in the freezer, and the rest of the ingredients kind of "came to me" while searching through the cabinets. The finished result was tender and juicy chops, with a nice pineapple flavor and a tiny bit of a kick in each bite.

TACO LASAGNA

serves 8

The Ingredients

1 pound lean ground beef, browned and drained

1 small onion, peeled and diced

1 green bell pepper, seeded and chopped

1 (1-ounce) packet taco seasoning (McCormick is gluten-free, or a homemade recipe is on page 27)

2/3 cup water

8 corn tortillas

1 (15-ounce) can refried beans

1 (15-ounce) can black beans, drained and rinsed

3 cups Mexican blend shredded cheese

tortilla chips, salsa, and sour cream (optional)

The Directions

Use a 4-quart slow cooker. Brown the meat on the stovetop with the onion and bell pepper. Drain the fat, and stir in the taco seasoning packet and water. Set aside.

Put 2 or 3 corn tortillas at the bottom of your stoneware (you'll need to tear and overlap them to cover the bottom completely). Smear on a bit of refried beans, then sprinkle on a handful of black beans. Top with a spoonful of the seasoned meat mixture and a scoop of shredded cheese. Repeat the layers until you run out of ingredients. Cover and cook on low for 5 to 6 hours, or on high for 2 to 3 hours. Serve with tortilla chips, salsa, and sour cream, if you'd like.

The Verdict

This is so tasty! My kids and a few of their friends (we had a playdate) had this for lunch, and Adam ate the leftovers cold when he came home from work. The tortillas get a bit soggy when slow cooked, but no one seemed to mind.

TERIYAKI AND APRICOT CHOPS

serves 4

The Ingredients

    4 pork chops
    2/3 cup apricot preserves
    1/4 cup teriyaki sauce (La Choy and Tamari Wheat-Free are gluten-free)
    1 teaspoon dried ginger
    2 tablespoons Dijon mustard

The Directions

Use a 4-quart slow cooker. Put the chops into your slow cooker. In a small bowl, mix together the rest of the ingredients and then pour evenly over the top of the chops. Cover and cook on low for 6 to 8 hours, or until the chops are thoroughly cooked and have reached the desired tenderness.

The Verdict

This is my husband's favorite pork chop recipe. We have brown rice or quinoa as a side, along with steamed broccoli.

TEX-MEX POT ROAST

serves 8

The Ingredients

    2 pounds boneless beef chuck roast
    1 teaspoon chipotle chile powder
    1 (15-ounce) can chili beans, undrained
    1 (11-ounce) can corn with peppers, drained
    1 (10-ounce) can tomatoes with chiles (Rotel), undrained

The Directions

Use a 6-quart slow cooker. This is a simple "dump it all in" recipe—my favorite kind. Put the meat into your cooker, and add the chile powder. Add the canned ingredients—be sure to drain off the corn juice. Cover and cook on low for 8 to 10 hours, high for 4 to 6 hours, or until the meat has reached the desired tenderness. If your meat isn't as tender as you'd like at dinnertime, remove it from the pot and cut it into a few pieces. Return to cook for another hour on high.

The Verdict

I served this meal with a baked potato to five adults and two children, and everyone really liked their dinner. Adding the beans and corn stretches an otherwise skimpy piece of meat into a filling meal for a houseful of people.

THAI BEEF

serves 4 to 6

The Ingredients

2 pounds beef chuck roast
1 (8-ounce) bottle peanut satay sauce (Thai Kitchen® is gluten-free)
1 (13.5-ounce) can coconut milk
1 (16-ounce) package baby carrots
cooked basmati rice for serving
¼ cup chopped peanuts as garnish (optional)

The Directions

Use a 6-quart slow cooker. Put the beef into the bottom of your slow cooker. Add the entire bottle of satay sauce and the can of coconut milk. Flip the meat over a few times to coat it nicely with the sauce. Add the baby carrots (I rinse them off first, even though the package says they're pre-washed). Cover and cook on low for 8 to 10 hours, or until the meat is fork-tender. Serve over basmati rice and garnish with chopped peanuts, if you'd like.

The Verdict

This is *so* good. The creaminess from the coconut milk balances out the satay sauce beautifully. I ate more than my fair share of this meat, and happily gobbled up the cold leftovers the next day. I was much too impatient to heat it up.

VENISON ROAST

serves 4 to 6

The Ingredients

    2 onions, sliced in rings
    $1/2$ teaspoon black pepper
    2 tablespoons gluten-free Worcestershire sauce
    2 pounds venison roast
    $1/2$ pound bacon
    1 cup beef broth
    $1/4$ cup butter, sliced, to add later

The Directions

Use a 6-quart slow cooker. Spread the onion rings around the bottom of your slow cooker insert. Rub the pepper and Worcestershire sauce directly onto the venison roast. Wrap the bacon strips around the meat, and place on top of the onions. Pour on the beef broth. Cover and cook on low for 6 to 7 hours, or until the meat has reached the desired tenderness. Slice the meat, and serve with a pat of butter.

The Verdict

Venison is a super lean meat, and you need to add a bit of fat to it while it's cooking. The bacon and butter balance the meat, and create a fantastic flavor and texture. Venison can dry out, but slow cooking really helps seal in all the juices. Thank you so much to our neighbor, Sherman, for the gift of this marvelous meat!

DESSERTS

Brandy Spiced Peaches   *281*

Chocolate-Almond Tapioca Pudding   *282*

Oreo Cookie Cheesecake   *283*

Red Wine–Poached Pears   *285*

Triple Chocolate Cake (aka Chocolate Mess)   *286*

Turtle Pudding   *287*

BRANDY SPICED PEACHES

serves 8

The Ingredients

2 (15-ounce) cans peach slices
2 tablespoons sugar
1 tablespoon apple cider vinegar
2 (3-inch) cinnamon sticks
1/2 teaspoon whole cloves
1/4 cup brandy
whipped cream as garnish (optional)

The Directions

Use a 2-quart slow cooker. Combine all the ingredients except for the brandy and whipped cream. Cook on low for 4 hours. Stir in the brandy. Refrigerate in a sealed plastic container for 48 hours, then remove the cinnamon sticks and cloves. Serve with a dollop of whipped cream, if desired.

The Verdict

This is my mom's friend Carol's traditional family Christmas dessert, and I can see why. It's marvelous. Carol wrote to me that the original recipe called for using canned peach halves, but there was too much "slipping and sliding" with the halves, so she now uses slices or pieces instead. The flavor is rich and pronounced, and you can definitely taste the brandy. This is not a recipe for children!

CHOCOLATE-ALMOND TAPIOCA PUDDING

serves 8 to 10

The Ingredients

    2 quarts 1 percent milk (half gallon)
    1½ cups sugar
    1 cup small pearl tapioca (not instant)
    3 large eggs
    1 teaspoon almond extract
    1 tablespoon cocoa powder

The Directions

Use a 4-quart slow cooker. Combine the milk, sugar, and tapioca in the stoneware insert. Stir well to mix. Cover and cook on high for 2 to 3 hours. You are looking for the tapioca to soften a bit and get slimy—it will still be very liquidy.

In a mixing bowl, whisk the eggs, almond extract, and cocoa powder together. Measure out ½ cup of the tapioca mixture from the crock, and whisk it into this egg mixture. Add another ½ cup of the tapioca mixture, and whisk that into the eggs, too. And then another! You are doing this to "temper" the eggs so they won't scramble when added to the slow cooker. Pour the egg mixture into the slow cooker, and stir well to combine. Cover and cook on high for 30 minutes to 1 hour, or until the tapioca has begun to swell and thicken.

Unplug the cooker, and leave the lid off for 1 hour while the tapioca cools. Your pudding will have become quite thick by now, and will be ready to chill in the refrigerator.

The Verdict

I thought I couldn't possibly love tapioca pudding any more than I already did, but then I tried this. The bit of cocoa powder and almond extract changes ordinary tapioca pudding from an afternoon snack to a sophisticated dessert.

OREO COOKIE CHEESECAKE

serves 6

The Ingredients

FOR THE CRUST

10 chocolate cream–filled sandwich cookies (I used Glutino brand)

3 tablespoons butter, melted

FOR THE FILLING

2 (8-ounce) blocks cream cheese, at room temperature

1/2 cup sugar

2 large eggs, at room temperature

1 tablespoon all-purpose flour (I used a gluten-free baking mix)

1/4 cup heavy cream

1 teaspoon vanilla extract

10 chocolate cream-filled sandwich cookies, crushed (I used Glutino brand)

The Directions

Use a 6-quart slow cooker and an oven-safe dish that can fit all the way into your stoneware for the cheesecake. You are going to create a bain-marie, or water bath. I used a 1½-quart Corningware dish and it fit perfectly inside of my 6-quart stoneware insert. In a zippered freezer bag, crush 10 of the chocolate sandwich cookies into tiny crumbs. Pour the melted butter into the bag, and squeeze the bag until the butter fully coats the crumbs. Press this crumb mixture into the bottom of your dish.

In a separate bowl, cream the cheese, sugar, eggs, flour, cream, and vanilla with a handheld or stand mixer. Stir in the crushed cookies. Pour the batter on top of the crust. Add 1/2 to 1 cup water to the bottom of your slow cooker, and slowly lower the dish into the stoneware, being careful not to slosh water into your cheesecake. Cover and cook on high for 2 to 3 hours, checking after 1 hour.

(CONTINUED)

Your cheesecake is done when the edges are no longer shiny and have begun to brown. Lightly touch the center to see if it has set.

Unplug the cooker. Let the cheesecake sit in the cooker for an hour before removing and transferring it to the refrigerator. Chill in the refrigerator completely before slicing and serving.

The Verdict

It's probably no surprise that my kids loved this. I have made about a dozen cheesecakes now in the slow cooker, and I'm always impressed with how well they turn out. The cakes are moist and gooey, and perfectly cooked. I will never again attempt cheesecake in the oven.

RED WINE–POACHED PEARS

serves 6

The Ingredients

2 (29-ounce) cans pear halves, drained
1 (750-ml) bottle red wine (I used an inexpensive merlot)
1 cup sugar
1 teaspoon vanilla extract
1 cinnamon stick
2 star anise
6 tablespoons sweetened whipped cream (the canned stuff)

The Directions

Use a 6-quart slow cooker. Drain pears, and put into your slow cooker. Add the entire bottle of wine and stir in the sugar, taking care to not break up the pear halves. Add the vanilla, and float the cinnamon stick and the star anise on top. Cover and cook on low for 5 hours, or high for 2 hours. Serve warm with a big dollop of whipped cream.

The Verdict

I ate a double portion of these pears to see if the alcohol cooks away. It does not. This is not a dessert for small children!

My mom's friend Carol sent me this recipe, which she got from an inn in Napa, California. The pears turn a lovely shade of purple, and are rich and delicious. I really liked the whipped cream on top, which melts instantly, creating a sweet creamy sauce.

TRIPLE CHOCOLATE CAKE (AKA CHOCOLATE MESS)

serves 8

The Ingredients

cooking spray
1 (16-ounce) package chocolate cake mix (I used Betty Crocker's Gluten-Free)
1 (4-ounce) package instant Jell-O® pudding mix
¾ cup canola or vegetable oil
1 cup water
4 eggs
1 (16-ounce) container sour cream
1 (6-ounce) package chocolate chips

The Directions

Use a 4-quart slow cooker. Spray the stoneware insert very well with cooking spray. In a large mixing bowl, combine the cake mix, pudding mix, oil, water, eggs, and sour cream. Beat with a hand mixer until light and fluffy. Stir in the chocolate chips. Scrape the batter into your prepared slow cooker. Cover and cook on low for 5 to 6 hours, or on high for 3 to 4 hours. Your cake will set on top, pull away from the sides, and an inserted toothpick will come out clean—just like a "real" cake!

The Verdict

Oh, my. Yum. This cake is like eating a hot chocolate volcano. The cake batter floats to the top, and the chocolate chips sink to create molten lava gooey fantastic goodness on the bottom. This recipe comes from Allison R., who says that she and her husband enjoy this cake warm with lots of vanilla ice cream.

TURTLE PUDDING

serves 8

The Ingredients

1 (16-ounce) box brownie mix (I used Betty Crocker's Gluten-Free)
1 large egg
¼ cup canola oil
¼ cup water
1 cup chocolate chips
½ cup chopped walnuts
20 wrapped soft caramels (unwrapped!)
whipped cream or vanilla ice cream for serving (optional)

The Directions

Use a 4- or 6-quart slow cooker with an inserted oven-safe dish. I used a round 4-quart cooker with a 2-quart inserted Corningware casserole dish. In a mixing bowl, combine the brownie mix, egg, oil, and water. When fully mixed, stir in the chocolate chips and walnuts. Pour the batter into your casserole dish. Push the caramel candies halfway into the brownie batter.

Add ½ to 1 cup water to the bottom of your slow cooker (you're using it as a bain-marie, or water bath), and lower in the dish. Cover and cook on high for 3 to 4 hours, or until the edges have pulled from the side and the center has set. Unplug, and let the dish sit in the slow cooker for 1 hour before removing. Serve warm with whipped cream or vanilla ice cream, if desired.

The Verdict

Super rich, and super satisfying. This is a terrific treat to make when you're craving chocolate.

Staples

*H*omemade versions of your favorite pantry and refrigerator staples.

Most of the recipes in this section (there are two new ones: Shredded Chicken and Vegetable Broth) appeared in the first *Make It Fast* cookbook. I've felt they are necessary to reprint because they are helpful to those trying to save money by cooking from scratch.

Baby Food   *291*

Beef Stock   *292*

Chicken Broth   *294*

Dry Beans   *296*

Marinara/Pasta Sauce   *298*

Shredded Chicken   *299*

Vegetable Broth   *300*

Yogurt   *301*

BABY FOOD

servings depend on amount of food cooked

The Ingredients

fresh or frozen fruit or vegetables
water

The Directions

Use a separate slow cooker for each variety of baby food. It's okay to use frozen fruit or vegetables. The food is picked at exactly the right time, and all nutrients are preserved perfectly during the freezing process. (I used yellow squash, sweet potatoes, and frozen green beans.) Wash and peel fresh vegetables. Cut into chunks, put into your slow cooker, and cover with the least amount of water needed to fully cook.

For the yellow squash, I used ¼ cup of water. For frozen green beans (toss in frozen), I used ¼ cup of water. For sweet potatoes, I ended up using ¾ cup of water.

Make baby food on a day you are home to monitor the food. Each variety will cook differently, depending on the moisture content and the density of the fruit or vegetable.

I used a 4-quart and two 6-quart slow cookers, and everything was cooked fully within 3 hours.

When the veggies or fruit are quite tender, unplug your cooker. Use a blender or a food processor to puree the food. If you need to add a bit of water to make it thinner for your baby, do so in little drips. Freeze in ice cube trays, then pop out and store in a freezer bag.

The Verdict

While I am writing this, I have a three-month-old baby in the house. She's not ready for baby food yet, but when she is, I'll be using this method to make her food—the same way I did for her sisters. I like picking out the biggest and brightest organic fruits and vegetables to turn into baby food. Choose in-season fruits and vegetables to save the most money.

BEEF STOCK

makes 3 quarts

The Ingredients

4 pounds oxtail, soup bones from a butcher, or bones/meat you've been saving for making broth
1 cup baby carrots
1 onion, chopped
1 bunch celery, chopped
8 garlic cloves, whole or chopped
1 tablespoon Italian seasoning
1 teaspoon kosher salt
1 teaspoon pepper
1 tablespoon apple cider vinegar

The Directions

Use a 6-quart slow cooker. This will take 2 days, so prepare yourself. Roast whatever meat and bones you are going to use on a high-sided cookie sheet in the oven at 400°F for 30 minutes. While the meat is roasting and releasing flavor, wash and coarsely chop the vegetables and put into the cooker. They do not need to look pretty. When the meat is done, let it cool a bit, then scrape into your crock. Include the juices. Add the spices, vinegar, and enough water to fill the rest of the crock minus 2 inches. Cover and cook on low for 10 to 12 hours. Let your slow cooker cool down on the countertop, then place the removable stoneware into the refrigerator overnight.

In the morning the fat will have floated to the top. It's quite gross. Discard the fat, and drain the broth with a colander into a large pot or bowl. Discard the bones and vegetables. Your stock is now ready to be used in your favorite soup or stew, and can be frozen for later use.

The Verdict

Although time consuming, homemade stock provides a flavorful punch to any recipe without excess salt or chemicals. Kalyn Denny, who writes kalynskitchen.blogspot.com, recommends saving meat scraps and bones for a few months in the freezer to use for broth, and using past-prime vegetables. This saves a lot of money.

CHICKEN BROTH

makes approximately 9 cups

The Ingredients

Carcass of 1 store-bought rotisserie chicken (or one you cooked yourself)
1 onion, chopped
1 cup chopped celery
2 cups chopped carrots
5 green onions, chopped
1 head garlic, peeled
3 bay leaves
1 tablespoon Italian seasoning
6 cups water

The Directions

Use a 6-quart slow cooker. This is a 2-day process, so plan accordingly. Put the chicken carcass into your slow cooker. Nestle the coarsely chopped vegetables in with the chicken bones. Add the garlic cloves, bay leaves, seasoning, and water. Cover and cook on low for 8 to 10 hours.

Remove the stoneware from the heating element and let cool completely. Wash your hands well, and find all the little chicken bones. Peel off and save any remaining chicken, and discard the bones and bay leaves. This is a good exercise in finding your inner nine-year-old.

Use a cup to scoop the soupy liquid into your blender to puree—do not discard the vegetables. When finished, pour the broth into zippered freezer bags in manageable portions. I chose to use 1-cup servings. Place the bags on a cookie sheet and freeze. Once the bags are frozen, they are small enough to be tucked in nooks around your freezer.

The Verdict

I'm not a purist, but I like to use my own broth when I have it on hand. Knowing exactly what is going into your family is important if you have allergies, health problems that call for low-sodium diets, or sensitivities to preservatives. This broth has no added salt, but has a bunch more flavor than store-bought. When using your homemade broth, add salt to taste.

DRY BEANS

makes approximately the same amount as 3 (15-ounce) cans

The Ingredients
1 pound dry beans
water

The Directions

Use a 6-quart slow cooker. Pour the dry beans into a colander and rinse under cold water. If you see any beans that have broken in half or skin that floats to the surface, get rid of it. Also pick out any beans that look shriveled or weird. Dump all the beans into your slow cooker, and add enough water to cover the beans completely and an additional 3 inches.

Cover. Do not turn the slow cooker on. Let the beans soak for at least 6 hours, or overnight. If you live in a very warm area and the slow cooker won't be in a room that is climate controlled, put the stoneware in the fridge. You don't want bacteria to have the opportunity to grow.

In the morning, dump the water and rinse the beans. If you are using kidney or red beans, you must boil the beans in fresh water on the stovetop for at least 10 minutes. Kidney and red beans can harbor a toxin and are unsafe if undercooked.

Put the beans back into your slow cooker and add enough fresh water to completely cover the beans by an extra 2 to 3 inches. Cover and cook on low for 8 to 10 hours, or until bite-tender. Don't worry if the water hasn't all been absorbed. Drain the beans.

When cool, put 1²/₃ cups of beans into storage containers or zippered freezer bags (you're adding this amount because you aren't adding filler liquid like cans have). The beans will store nicely in the refrigerator for 1 week or in the freezer for 6 months. Use as you would canned beans in your favorite recipe.

The Verdict

One bag of dry black beans costs $1.89 at our fancy-pants grocery store, and $0.89 at our local produce stand. A can of organic black beans at Trader Joe's costs $0.99. One pound of dried beans equals 3 (15-ounce) cans of beans. This means that even if you buy expensive dry beans, you will save some money making them at home yourself. I like knowing what is in my food, and I like the idea that we can save money and reduce garbage by using dry beans.

MARINARA/PASTA SAUCE

makes approximately 9 cups

The Ingredients

1 pound lean ground meat, browned and drained (optional)
1 (28-ounce) can whole peeled tomatoes
1 (12.5-ounce) can Italian diced tomatoes
1 (15-ounce) can tomato sauce
1 tablespoon Italian seasoning, plus more to taste
1 pound mushrooms, sliced

The Directions

Use a 6-quart slow cooker. Add the browned ground meat, if using, to your slow cooker. Dump in tomatoes with their liquid and the tomato sauce. Stir in the Italian seasoning and mushrooms. Cover and cook on low for 8 to 10 hours. When the cooking time has elapsed, taste the sauce. Add more Italian seasoning if needed.

Bottled pasta sauce is awfully salty. I don't add any salt when I make my own, but your tongue might desperately want you to. Serve right away, or package for freezing.

The Verdict

There aren't any rules when it comes to making marinara sauce—use tomatoes from your garden or whatever's on sale at the supermarket, and feel free to add lots of garlic.

SHREDDED CHICKEN

When whole chickens or chicken quarters go on sale (sometimes as low as $0.57 a pound!), I like to buy a lot to cook for "naked chicken"—which is cooked shredded chicken to have on hand for lunches, snacks, and dinners.

. . . .

What I do:

The chicken I get on sale is bone-in and has skin. I trim off as much of the skin as I possibly can, and throw the skinned pieces into a large slow cooker. I can fit about 8 quarters into a 6-quart slow cooker.

I typically do not add any seasoning, nor do I add cooking liquid such as water or broth. I simply put the lid on and let it cook on low for 6 to 8 hours, or until the meat is fully cooked and falls away from the bones. If your particular slow cooker releases a lot of condensation through a vent hole or gap around the lid, put a layer of foil or parchment paper down over the stoneware, and then re-place the lid. This will trap all the moisture and heat inside the pot.

When the cooking time has elapsed, I take the lid off and let the chicken cool quite a bit before handling.

I fish out the bones and chicken, and save the cooked, naked chicken to freeze for later use. The juice left in the bottom of the pot is enough to use as a soup base or chicken broth. See page 36 for Old-Fashioned Chicken Noodle Soup or page 294 for homemade chicken broth.

STAPLES

VEGETABLE BROTH

makes approximately 4 quarts

The Ingredients
vegetable peels
odds and ends from vegetables
water
salt (I do not add salt now, but instead add to taste when I use the broth in a recipe)

The Directions
Use a 6-quart slow cooker. This is actually a "free" recipe! When cooking, save your vegetable peels and the trimmed-off pieces. In order for this to be safe, you will need to wash your vegetables very well and scrub off all the dirt. I highly recommend choosing organic vegetables, or even better, organic vegetables that you've grown in your own garden.

Many people keep a large Tupperware container in their freezer, or a plastic zippered bag to contain the peels and scraps until cooking time. Carrot peels, onion skin, celery ends, bell pepper stems, and garlic skins are wonderful broth-making ingredients to save. Don't bother with potato skin—it's too starchy and has an overwhelming earthy flavor.

Put the (washed) vegetable peels and odds and ends into your slow cooker. Cover with water—I don't really measure; I just fill the crock up to about 3 inches from the top. Cover and cook on low 10 to 12 hours. Place a colander into a large stockpot, and carefully strain the vegetable pieces from your broth into the pot. Cool completely and freeze in plastic containers or zippered freezer bags until you are ready to use in your favorite recipe.

The Verdict
It's very interesting to me how the garlic and onion peels infuse the water with so much flavor. You can tweak your broth to taste like your favorite ingredients. If you want more of a garlic flavor, save more garlic wrappers, and so on. If you use even the smallest amount of beet skin, you will get red broth. Neat!

YOGURT

serves 12

The Ingredients

8 cups (half gallon) whole milk—pasteurized and homogenized is fine, but do not use ultra-pasteurized.

1/2 cup natural live/active culture plain yogurt

thick bath towel

1 (0.3-ounce) packet unflavored gelatin (optional)

1/2 cup nonfat dry milk (optional)

colander

2 coffee filters

frozen/fresh fruit for flavoring (optional)

1 (1.4-ounce) box instant pudding mix (optional)

The Directions

Use a 4-quart slow cooker. This takes a while; make yogurt on a day when you are home to monitor. Plug in your slow cooker and turn to low. Add the milk. Cover and cook on low for 2 1/2 hours. Unplug your cooker, leave the cover on, and let it sit for 3 hours. When time has passed, scoop out 2 cups of the warmish milk to put in a bowl. Whisk in 1/2 cup of the live/active culture yogurt. Then dump the bowl contents back into the crock. Stir to combine. Put the lid back on your slow cooker. Keep it unplugged, and wrap a heavy bath towel all the way around the crock for insulation.

Go to bed, or let it sit for 8 hours. In the morning, the yogurt will have thickened—it's not as thick as store-bought yogurt, but it has the consistency of plain low-fat yogurt. If desired, stir in a packet of unflavored gelatin or some nonfat dry milk into your yogurt to help it thicken. Line a colander with coffee filters, and pour in the yogurt. After a few hours, the whey will have separated and you'll be left with lovely yogurt. Stir in fresh or frozen fruit, if desired, or a box of pudding mix.

(CONTINUED)

Chill in a plastic container(s) in the refrigerator. Your fresh yogurt will last 7 to 10 days. Save ½ cup as a starter to make a new batch.

The Verdict

Wowsers! This is awesome! I was completely astonished the next morning that the yogurt had thickened. I was so excited to feel the drag on the spoon—I scared the kids with my squealing. This recipe has been tried many times by readers of my Web site, and many like the thickness provided by the gelatin and/or nonfat dry milk. If your house gets rather chilly at nighttime, your yogurt will not set as well. My house was about 65°F.

ACKNOWLEDGMENTS

This book is a group effort. I would not have been able to cook and write about all of the recipes without help. I am forever grateful to my family, who took so much time out of their busy lives to help with food shopping and preparation, taste testing, baby wrangling, and help getting my big kids to school and home again.

Thank you so much to my Grandma Bunny and my fabulous father-in-law, John, for coming over every single day for four months to play with our new baby while I cooked and wrote.

Thank you to my mom for reading every single word. And then reading them over again.

Thank you to my dad, Andy, Karen, and Grandpa Ken for helping us eat so much food, and for your indispensable feedback and support.

Thank you to my three girls, and to my wonderful husband, Adam, for your patience, love, and hand-holding.

Thank you to my amazing readers and friends who took the time to write and suggest new recipes. Your love and support means so very much.

Thank you to the following people who helped bring the *Make It Fast*, *Cook It Slow* cookbooks to life:

Alison Picard
Ellen Archer
Barbara A. Jones
Leslie Wells
Elisabeth Dyssegaard
Allison McGeehon
Ed and Allison O'Keefe

Thank you to the following Web sites for your help and inspiration:

5dollardinners.com

BlogHer.com

glutenfreeeasily.com

glutenfreegirl.blogspot.com

glutenfreegoddess.blogspot.com

kalynskitchen.blogspot.com

ninecooks.typepad.com

pastaqueen.com

surefoodsliving.com

thepioneerwoman.com

thewholegang.org

threekidcircus.com

todayscreativeblog.blogspot.com

whatscookingblog.com

wouldashoulda.com

ACKNOWLEDGMENTS

INDEX

A

almond(s):
-chocolate tapioca pudding, 282
ginger chicken, 248
raisin nut oatmeal, 115
sugared cinnamon, 199
wasabi, 124
appetizers:
apricot barbecue wings, 212
baked herbed feta, 24
beer and cheddar fondue, 213
big barbecue Little Smokies, 120
double artichoke dip, 121
fruit and horseradish cream cheese
spread, 122
grape jelly and chili sauce Little
Smokies, 25
meatballs in peanut chili sauce, 214
orange-glazed meatballs, 123
pineapple party meatballs, 215
ranch party mix, 26
taco dip, 27–28
thyme for goat cheese, 29
wasabi almonds, 124
apple(s):
candied acorn squash, 55
caramel fondue, 96
caramel spiced cider, 16
coffee cake, 194–95
halves, baked maple, 95
multigrain porridge, 21
-pecan bread pudding, 113–14
scalloped, 102
stuffing with sausage and, 236

apricot(s):
barbecue wings, 212
chicken with dates and, 165
-glazed pork roast, 255
and teriyaki chops, 276
artichoke:
dip, double, 121
pasta, 153

B

baby food, 291
bacon:
potluck beans, 230
ultimate breakfast casserole,
117–18
banana maple oat bread, 208–9
basil:
Herb, the catfish, 159
pesto chicken and sweet potatoes
layered dinner, 174–75
pesto lasagna, 154
pesto minestrone soup, 225
bean(s), 13
baked, soup, 42–43
black, with cilantro, 44
and cheese burrito casserole, 69
chicken enchilada chili, 138
chili macaroni and cheese, 180
and corn soup, smoky, 39
cowboy, 49–50
dry, 296–97
end of summer harvest soup, 33–34
green, creamy turkey and, 247

hoppin' John, 51
Indian spiced lentils with chicken,
139–40
lentil soup, 35
minestrone soup, 130
Moroccan chicken with lentils,
86
pepperoni pizza chili, 141
pesto minestrone soup, 225
pineapple baked, 142
poor man's chili, 52
pork and, "real," 229
potluck, 230
red, and rice, coconut, 45–46
sloppy lentils, 143
and smoked sausage stew, 144
soup, calico, 47–48
succotash, 66
sweet potato chili (vegan!), 231
taco lasagna, 275
Tex-Mex pot roast, 277
vegetable-stuffed peppers, 79
vegetarian baked, 53
vegetarian chili shepherd's pie, 80
vegetarian tortilla soup, 134–35
white, Italian chili, 228
zesty burger soup, 40
beef:
Asian shredded, 256–57
big easy meatloaf, 178–79
bourguignon, 258–59
chili macaroni and cheese, 180
cowboy beans, 49–50
Dijon corned, 260
dry rub ribs, 181

beef (continued)
  ground, layered casserole, 90
  Hawaiian barbecue ribs, 261
  juicy burgers, 89
  leftovers for breakfast, 20
  loose meat sandwiches, 264
  macaroni and (American chop suey), 254
  old-fashioned pot roast, 266
  orange, 267
  peperoncini, sandwiches, 185
  pepperoni pizza chili, 141
  puffy pizza casserole, 269–70
  ravioli lasagna, 272
  simple pepper steak, 187
  snowy day ribs, 273
  stew, Hungarian, 127
  stock, 292–93
  super simple cranberry roast, 188
  sweet and savory pot roast, 189
  sweet mustard roast, 190
  taco lasagna, 275
  taco pie, 191–92
  Tex-Mex pot roast, 277
  Thai, 278
  zesty burger soup, 40
beer:
  and cheddar fondue, 213
  cheese soup, 218
beets, orange-glazed, 150
beverages:
  Boston tea punch, 204
  caramel apple spiced cider, 16
  Caribbean coffee, 205
  coconut hot chocolate, 109
  Irish coffee, 17
  luncheon lemonade, 18
  witch's brew, 110–11
bok choy:
  ginger tilapia with, 157
  orange beef, 267
brandy spiced peaches, 281
bread:
  maple banana oat, 208–9
  pudding, apple-pecan, 113–14
  stuffing with apple and sausage, 236
  ultimate breakfast casserole, 117–18

breakfasts:
  apple-pecan bread pudding, 113–14
  cheesy sausage bake, 207
  leftovers for, 20
  maple banana oat bread, 208–9
  multigrain porridge, 21
  raisin nut oatmeal, 115
  sausage and tomato casserole, 210
  southwestern hash brown bake, 116
  steel cut oatmeal, 22
  ultimate casserole, 117–18
broth, 7, 107
  chicken, 294–95
  vegetable, 300
brussels sprouts, best, 146
burrito casserole, bean and cheese, 69

C

cake:
  coffee, apple, 194–95
  lemon pudding, 98
  peanut butter cup, 100–101
  triple chocolate (aka chocolate mess), 286
caramel:
  apple spiced cider, 16
  fondue, 96
  turtle pudding, 287
carnitas, 88
carrot(s), 7
  dill baby, 149
  pioneer dinner, 92
  pudding, 147
  roasted root vegetables, 63
  sweet and savory pot roast, 189
casseroles, 14
  bean and cheese burrito, 69
  layered ground beef, 90
  puffy pizza, 269–70
  sausage and tomato breakfast, 210
  spinach, 235
  ultimate breakfast, 117–18
catfish:
  Herb the, 159
  Italian, 240

cauliflower gratin, 148
cheese:
  baked chicken with feta and fennel, 243
  baked herbed feta, 24
  baked potato soup, 31
  and bean burrito casserole, 69
  beer and cheddar fondue, 213
  beer soup, 218
  cauliflower gratin, 148
  chili macaroni and, 180
  cream, and fruit and horseradish spread, 122
  creamed corn, 233
  creamy ranch mashed red potatoes, 56–57
  eggplant Parmesan, 72–73
  enchilada stack, 70–71
  goat, thyme for, 29
  layered ground beef casserole, 90
  leftovers for breakfast, 20
  Oreo cookie cheesecake, 283–84
  pesto lasagna, 154
  pizza chicken, 176
  pizza potatoes, 151
  potatoes au Gruyère, 234
  ravioli lasagna, 272
  sausage breakfast bake, 207
  "scalloped" potatoes, 64
  southwestern hash brown bake, 116
  spinach bisque, 131
  spinach casserole, 235
  taco dip, 27–28
  taco lasagna, 275
  taco pie, 191–92
  ultimate breakfast casserole, 117–18
  vegetable-stuffed peppers, 79
  vegetarian chili shepherd's pie, 80
cheesecake, Oreo cookie, 283–84
Chex cereal:
  ranch party mix, 26
  sticky dessert, 103
chicken:
  African peanut stew, 217
  apricot barbecue wings, 212
  with apricots and dates, 165
  baked, with feta and fennel, 243
  big bayou jambalaya, 219–20
  broth, 294–95

cacciatore, 164
country captain, 245–46
easy peanut butter, 82
enchilada chili, 138
General Tso's, 83
ginger almond, 248
green pepper, 166–67
herb garden, 168
herb-roasted, with summer tomatoes,
169–70
honey garlic, 84
Indian spiced lentils with, 139–40
korma, 244
lean, mean and green tortilla soup,
128
leftovers for breakfast, 20
marmalade curry, 85
Moroccan, with lentils, 86
mulligatawny, 222
noodle soup, old-fashioned, 36–37
pad Thai, 249–50
pizza, 176
shredded, 299
stew, Ethiopian, 126
sweet garlic barbecue, 251
white wine coq au vin, 252
chili:
    chicken enchilada, 138
    Italian white bean, 228
    macaroni and cheese, 180
    pepperoni pizza, 141
    poor man's, 52
    sweet potato (vegan!), 231
    vegetarian, shepherd's pie, 80
chocolate:
    -almond tapioca pudding, 282
    cake, triple (aka chocolate mess), 286
    hot, coconut, 109
    mint fondue, 99
    peanut butter cup cake, 100–101
    pot de crème with ganache, 196
    turtle pudding, 287
cider, caramel apple spiced, 16
cilantro, black beans with, 44
cinnamon:
    almonds, sugared, 199
    raisin rice pudding, 97

clam chowder:
    Manhattan, 129
    New England, 223–24
coconut:
    hot chocolate, 109
    meatballs in peanut chili sauce, 214
    red beans and rice, 45–46
coffee:
    Caribbean, 205
    Irish, 17
coffee cake, apple, 194–95
corn:
    and bean soup, smoky, 39
    cheesy creamed, 233
    and crab soup, 221
    lean, mean and green tortilla soup, 128
    poor man's chili, 52
    succotash, 66
    Tex-Mex pot roast, 277
    turkey stew, 132–33
    vegetarian chili shepherd's pie, 80
    zesty burger soup, 40
country captain, 245–46
crab and corn soup, 221
cranberry(ies):
    fruit and horseradish cream cheese
    spread, 122
    roast, super simple, 188
curry marmalade chicken, 85
custard, vanilla, 104

D

dates, chicken with apricots and, 165
desserts:
    apple coffee cake, 194–95
    baked maple apple halves, 95
    brandy spiced peaches, 281
    caramel fondue, 96
    chocolate-almond tapioca pudding,
    282
    chocolate pot de crème with ganache,
    196
    cinnamon raisin rice pudding, 97
    holiday pears, 197
    lemon pudding cake, 98

mint chocolate fondue, 99
Oreo cookie cheesecake, 283–84
peanut butter cup cake, 100–101
raspberry fondue, 198
red wine-poached pears, 285
scalloped apples, 102
sticky cereal, 103
sugared cinnamon almonds, 199
triple chocolate cake (aka chocolate
mess), 286
turtle pudding, 287
vanilla custard, 104
dill:
    baby carrots, 149
    Herb, the catfish, 159
dips:
    double artichoke, 121
    taco, 27–28

E

eggplant Parmesan, 72–73
eggs:
    Ethiopian chicken stew, 126
    leftovers for breakfast, 20
    ultimate breakfast casserole, 117–18
enchilada:
    chili, chicken, 138
    stack, cheese, 70–71

F

fennel:
    baked chicken with feta and, 243
    Greek fish in foil, 158
fish and seafood:
    big bayou jambalaya, 219–20
    country captain, 245–46
    crab and corn soup, 221
    ginger tilapia with bok choy, 157
    Greek fish in foil, 158
    Herb, the catfish, 159
    Italian catfish, 240
    Manhattan clam chowder, 129
    New England clam chowder, 223–24
    orange and honey tilapia, 160

fish and seafood *(continued)*
    salmon loaf, 161–62
    salmon with lime butter, 241
fondues:
    beer and cheddar, 213
    caramel, 96
    mint chocolate, 99
    raspberry, 198
freezer staples, 7–8

G

garlic:
    barbecue chicken, sweet, 251
    honey chicken, 84
    red potatoes with rosemary and, 61
    roasted, spoonbread, 62
ginger:
    almond chicken, 248
    and pear pork chops, 184
    tilapia with bok choy, 157
gluten-free foods, 5–6
grape jelly and chili sauce Little Smokies, 25
green beans, creamy turkey and, 247

H

ham:
    honey-glazed, with thyme, 262
    leftovers for breakfast, 20
herb(s), 107
    the catfish, 159
    garden chicken, 168
    -roasted chicken with summer tomatoes,
        169–70
honey:
    garlic chicken, 84
    -glazed ham with thyme, 262
    and orange tilapia, 160
hoppin' John, 51
horseradish and fruit cream cheese spread,
    122

J

jambalaya, big bayou, 219–20

L

lamb, leg of, with rosemary and lemon,
    263
lasagna:
    pesto, 154
    ravioli, 272
    taco, 275
lemon:
    baked tofu, 74
    leg of lamb with rosemary and, 263
    pudding cake, 98
lemonade, luncheon, 18
lentil(s):
    Indian spiced, with chicken, 139–40
    Moroccan chicken with, 86
    sloppy, 143
    soup, 35
lime butter, salmon with, 241

M

macaroni:
    and beef (American chop suey), 254
    and cheese, chili, 180
maple:
    apple halves, baked, 95
    banana oat bread, 208–9
    -glazed pork chops, 91
marinara/pasta sauce, 298
marmalade curry chicken, 85
meal planning, 6
meat:
    ground, 7
    honey-glazed ham with thyme, 262
    leftovers for breakfast, 20
    leg of lamb with rosemary and lemon,
        263
    marinara/pasta sauce, 298
    meatballs in peanut chili sauce, 214
    orange-glazed meatballs, 123
    pineapple party meatballs, 215
    portion sizes of, 13–14
    potluck beans, 230
    ultimate breakfast casserole, 117–18
    venison roast, 279
    see also beef; pork; sausage

meatballs:
    orange-glazed, 123
    in peanut chili sauce, 214
    pineapple party, 215
meatloaf, big easy, 178–79
minestrone soup, 130
    pesto, 225
mint chocolate fondue, 99
money-saving shortcuts, 6–9
mulligatawny, 222
mushroom(s):
    pork chops, 265
    portobello, sandwiches, 75
    teriyaki portobello, 155
mustard:
    Dijon corned beef, 260
    roast, sweet, 190

O

oat(s):
    bread, maple banana, 208–9
    multigrain porridge, 21
    raisin nut oatmeal, 115
    steel cut oatmeal, 22
onions, 7
    steak and, tofu, 76
orange:
    beef, 267
    -glazed beets, 150
    -glazed meatballs, 123
    and honey tilapia, 160
    marmalade curry chicken, 85

P

pad Thai, 249–50
pantry staples, 7–8
party mix, ranch, 26
pasta:
    American chop suey (macaroni and
        beef), 254
    artichoke, 153
    chili macaroni and cheese, 180
    pesto lasagna, 154
    ravioli lasagna, 272

pasta/marinara sauce, 298
pea, yellow split, soup with smoked paprika,
    136
peaches, brandy spiced, 281
peanut (butter):
    chicken, easy, 82
    chili sauce, meatballs in, 214
    cup cake, 100–101
    Indonesian pork, 268
    stew, African, 217
pear(s):
    and ginger pork chops, 184
    holiday, 197
    red wine-poached, 285
peperoncini beef sandwiches, 185
pepper(s), bell:
    big bayou jambalaya, 219–20
    green, chicken, 166–67
    Hungarian beef stew, 127
    Italian catfish, 240
    orange beef, 267
    steak, simple, 187
    vegetable-stuffed, 79
pepperoni:
    pizza chili, 141
    pizza potatoes, 151
pesto:
    chicken and sweet potatoes layered
        dinner, 174–75
    lasagna, 154
    minestrone soup, 225
pineapple:
    baked beans, 142
    chops, spicy, 274
    party meatballs, 215
    peanut butter Indonesian pork, 268
    sweet potatoes, 60
pioneer dinner, 92
pizza:
    casserole, puffy, 269–70
    chicken, 176
    pepperoni, chili, 141
    potatoes, 151
pork:
    Asian shredded, 256–57
    and beans, "real," 229
    carnitas, 88

chops, maple-glazed, 91
chops, mushroom, 265
chops, pear and ginger, 184
dry rub ribs, 181
Greek ribs, 182–83
honey-glazed ham with thyme, 262
leftovers for breakfast, 20
peanut butter Indonesian, 268
pulled, with sauerkraut, 271
roast, apricot-glazed, 255
root beer pulled, 186
spicy pineapple chops, 274
sticky chops, 93
super simple cranberry roast, 188
sweet mustard roast, 190
teriyaki and apricot chops, 276
porridge, multigrain, 21
portion sizes, 13–14
potato(es):
    baked, soup, 31
    cheesy sausage breakfast bake, 207
    creamy ranch mashed red, 56–57
    au Gruyère, 234
    Irish, 58
    layered ground beef casserole, 90
    leftovers for breakfast, 20
    New England clam chowder, 223–24
    old-fashioned pot roast, 266
    pesto minestrone soup, 225
    pioneer dinner, 92
    pizza, 151
    red, with rosemary and garlic, 61
    roasted root vegetables, 63
    scalloped, 64
    southwestern hash brown bake, 116
    vegetarian chili shepherd's pie, 80
pot de crème with ganache, chocolate, 196
poultry, see chicken; turkey
pudding:
    apple-pecan bread, 113–14
    cake, lemon, 98
    carrot, 147
    chocolate-almond tapioca, 282
    cinnamon raisin rice, 97
    turtle, 287
    vanilla custard, 104
punch, Boston tea, 204

R

raisin:
    cinnamon rice pudding, 97
    nut oatmeal, 115
raspberry fondue, 198
ravioli lasagna, 272
rice:
    coconut red beans and, 45–46
    country captain, 245–46
    Italian, 59
    multigrain porridge, 21
    pudding, cinnamon raisin, 97
    sun-dried tomato risotto, 238
    vegetable-stuffed peppers, 79
risotto, sun-dried tomato, 238
root beer pulled pork, 186
rosemary:
    herb garden chicken, 168
    leg of lamb with lemon and, 263
    red potatoes with garlic and, 61

S

salmon:
    with lime butter, 241
    loaf, 161–62
sandwiches:
    juicy beefy burgers, 89
    loose meat, 264
    not-so-sloppy joes, 173
    peperoncini beef, 185
    portobello mushroom, 75
    sloppy lentils, 143
sauce, marinara/pasta, 298
sauerkraut:
    pulled pork with, 271
    soup, 38
sausage(s):
    big barbecue Little Smokies, 120
    big bayou jambalaya, 219–20
    big easy meatloaf, 178–79
    cheesy breakfast bake, 207
    grape jelly and chili sauce Little Smokies,
    25
    hoppin' John, 51
    Italian white bean chili, 228

sausage(s) *(continued)*
    pepperoni pizza chili, 141
    pioneer dinner, 92
    pizza potatoes, 151
    smoked, and bean stew, 144
    southwestern hash brown bake, 116
    stuffing with apple and, 236
    sweet potato and chorizo soup, 226
    and tomato breakfast casserole, 210
seafood, *see* fish and seafood
shepherd's pie, vegetarian chili, 80
shrimp:
    big bayou jambalaya, 219–20
    country captain, 245–46
side dishes:
    best brussels sprouts, 146
    candied acorn squash, 55
    carrot pudding, 147
    cauliflower gratin, 148
    cheesy creamed corn, 233
    creamy ranch mashed red potatoes,
    56–57
    dill baby carrots, 149
    Irish potatoes, 58
    Italian rice, 59
    orange-glazed beets, 150
    pineapple sweet potatoes, 60
    pizza potatoes, 151
    potatoes au Gruyère, 234
    red potatoes with rosemary and garlic,
    61
    roasted garlic spoonbread, 62
    roasted root vegetables, 63
    "scalloped" potatoes, 64
    spaghetti squash, 65
    spinach casserole, 235
    stuffing with apple and sausage, 236
    succotash, 66
    sun-dried tomato risotto, 238
sloppy joes, not-so-, 173
sloppy lentils, 143
slow cooker, choosing, 9
soups, 13, 14
    baked bean, 42–43
    baked potato, 31
    beer cheese, 218
    calico bean, 47–48

crab and corn, 221
creamy tomato, 32
end of summer harvest, 33–34
lean, mean and green tortilla, 128
lentil, 35
Manhattan clam chowder, 129
minestrone, 130
mulligatawny, 222
New England clam chowder, 223–24
old-fashioned chicken noodle, 36–37
pesto minestrone, 225
sauerkraut, 38
smoky bean and corn, 39
spinach bisque, 131
sweet potato and chorizo, 226
vegetarian tortilla, 134–35
yellow split pea, with smoked paprika,
136
zesty burger, 40
spices, 6–7
spinach:
    bisque, 131
    casserole, 235
    minestrone soup, 130
    pesto lasagna, 154
split pea, yellow, soup with smoked paprika,
136
spoonbread, roasted garlic, 62
spreads:
    baked herbed feta, 24
    fruit and horseradish cream cheese,
    122
    thyme for goat cheese, 29
squash:
    candied acorn, 55
    end of summer harvest soup, 33–34
    spaghetti, 65
staples:
    baby food, 291
    beef stock, 292–93
    chicken broth, 294–95
    dry beans, 296–97
    marinara/pasta sauce, 298
    pantry and freezer items, 7–8
    shredded chicken, 299
    vegetable broth, 300
    yogurt, 301-2

stews, 13
    African peanut, 217
    big bayou jambalaya, 219–20
    Ethiopian chicken, 126
    Hungarian beef, 127
    smoked sausage and bean, 144
    turkey, 132–33
stock, 7
    beef, 292–93
stuffing with apple and sausage, 236
succotash, 66
sweet potato(es):
    African peanut stew, 217
    chili (vegan!), 231
    and chorizo soup, 226
    old-fashioned chicken noodle soup,
    36–37
    pesto chicken and, layered dinner, 174–75
    pineapple, 60
    roasted root vegetables, 63
    turkey stew, 132–33

T

taco:
    dip, 27–28
    lasagna, 275
    pie, 191–92
tapioca pudding, chocolate-almond, 282
tea punch, Boston, 204
thyme:
    for goat cheese, 29
    Herb, the catfish, 159
    herb garden chicken, 168
    honey-glazed ham with, 262
tilapia:
    ginger, with bok choy, 157
    orange and honey, 160
tofu, 13
    baked, 68
    "fish" cakes, 77–78
    lemon baked, 74
    steak and onions, 76
tomato(es), 107
    end of summer harvest soup, 33–34
    poor man's chili, 52

and sausage breakfast casserole, 210
succotash, 66
summer, herb-roasted chicken with, 169–70
tomato, sun-dried, risotto, 238
tomatoes, canned:
African peanut stew, 217
American chop suey (macaroni and beef), 254
artichoke pasta, 153
baked bean soup, 42–43
bean and cheese burrito casserole, 69
big bayou jambalaya, 219–20
calico bean soup, 47–48
cheese enchilada stack, 70–71
chicken cacciatore, 164
chicken enchilada chili, 138
chicken korma, 244
chili macaroni and cheese, 180
country captain, 245–46
cowboy beans, 49–50
Ethiopian chicken stew, 126
hoppin' John, 51
Italian rice, 59
Italian white bean chili, 228
lentil soup, 35
Manhattan clam chowder, 129

marinara/pasta sauce, 298
minestrone soup, 130
mulligatawny, 222
pepperoni pizza chili, 141
pesto minestrone soup, 225
"real" pork and beans, 229
sauerkraut soup, 38
simple pepper steak, 187
soup, creamy, 32
sweet garlic barbecue chicken, 251
sweet potato chili (vegan!), 231
Tex-Mex pot roast, 277
turkey stew, 132–33
vegetarian tortilla soup, 134–35
zesty burger soup, 40
tortilla(s):
bean and cheese burrito casserole, 69
cheese enchilada stack, 70–71
soup, lean, mean and green, 128
soup, vegetarian, 134–35
taco lasagna, 275
turkey:
big easy meatloaf, 178–79
cowboy beans, 49–50
and green beans, creamy, 247
Japanese takeout, 171–72
loose meat sandwiches, 264
not-so-sloppy joes, 173
stew, 132–33

V

vanilla custard, 104
vegetable broth, 300
vegetarian main courses:
artichoke pasta, 153
baked tofu, 68
bean and cheese burrito casserole, 69
cheese enchilada stack, 70–71
chili shepherd's pie, 80
eggplant Parmesan, 72–73
lemon baked tofu, 74
pesto lasagna, 154
portobello mushroom sandwiches, 75
steak and onions tofu, 76
teriyaki portobello mushrooms, 155
tofu "fish" cakes, 77–78
vegetable-stuffed peppers, 79
venison roast, 279

W

wasabi almonds, 124
witch's brew, 110–11

Y

yogurt, 301–2